CW01460698

Strategy
for
Credit
Unions

A guide for Management and Boards

First published 2016 by Alan Shaw

Cover design and layout by OneStopPrinting.ie

Acknowledgments

This book would not have materialised were it not for the help and initiative of a few good people.

In chronological order I would like to express my thanks to the board of 2010, including Sarah and Arthur who decided that Strategy was a subject matter worth developing in our Credit Union. Thus embarking on a voyage of discovery with initial guidance from Bert Farrell and Kieran Horan. Both of these gentlemen helped us to appreciate the benefits of strategic thinking, and whetted our appetites for what was to follow.

To CEO, Mick Culkeen, who is a strategist to the core, and I am sure there is a book or two in him! He encouraged me to step out of my comfort zone last year, and invited me to 'sharpen my saw' as Stephen Covey would say.

My Credit Union board deserves acknowledgement for the support they so readily give to me. They have always allowed me the freedom to develop new concepts and initiatives.

I hadn't known that writing and publishing a book was within my grasp until my brother Ken told me he had written a 500 pager and published it on a well known website. That gave me the interest and belief I needed to take the first step here.

Special thanks to my work colleagues, Ann Marie, Shona, and Martina and Martina who provided the proof-reading and feedback that every book undergoes to make it presentable to the reader.

I am indebted to my heirs, Fiona and Robert. They are an inspiration and have helped me with some of the detail I was missing. Always supportive in whatever I do, yet busy getting on with their own hectic lives. I am grateful to Fiona for her powerful command of the English language and the time she afforded me in polishing my act, and to Robert for his insightful understanding of the technical content.

Last but not least to my wife Dympna, who has always been there while I was snowed under with books and papers. The days away on study, and the many evenings tapping on the keyboard would have got the better of some. But she is used to my tapping at this stage. Thank you for the countless cups of tea and for being there.

Preface

The first question I need to answer for you is:

> 'Will I benefit from reading this book, as I am not a CEO or board member.........yet?'

It's pretty clear that if you are a Credit Union CEO, or if you are part of the management team, then, yes, you probably need to better understand strategy.

Likewise if you are serving as a board member or are in a voluntary capacity with your Credit Union, it's useful to be capable of joining in the conversation when discussing the future of your organisation.

For employees who have a desire to be closer to the decision making process, and believe that you have a vested interest in the Credit Union you rely on for your income, I expect that you will gain a significant advantage by owning and reading this book.

Because we are talking Credit Unions, I have kept the conversation somewhat local. It will be evident to you that my Credit Union is based in Ireland, but the same narrative applies wherever you are based.

Although I address the CEO throughout the book, please note that this is more for convenience. Whatever your position you should consider yourself as the singular audience as you read through the following chapters.

About the Author

I have the honour of serving members in a large Credit Union in Ireland. In Irish terms that's assets above €100m. During my time here I have been immersed in the development and review of the strategic plan, participated and led in new product development, and represented the managers forum in the west of the country. I have also visited Brussels with Marian Harkin, MEP to look at new lending options for Credit Unions in Ireland.

Recently, I completed a Diploma in Strategy and Innovation at the Irish Management Institute, which has broadened my horizons on the subject of strategy.

Previous endeavours included building and opening a 100-seater restaurant, as owner/manager for eleven years. It was opened the year the Celtic Tiger took off and closed in tandem with the same Tiger's demise! We had clearly defined points of differentiation for the business, and whilst we didn't know it at the time we were working off an unwritten strategy. Even the exit from the business was strategically planned so as to protect reputations and suppliers.

A large part of my early career was in AIB retail banking in the UK. We referred to ourselves as 'pioneers' in the 1970's and 80's, as we were building a business from scratch, and opening new branches every few months. Having progressed through the management functions in retail banking, I worked with executives in HQ, formulating strategies on marketing and business development. They asked me to travel the length and breadth of Britain in search of joint venture partners, and this was the time of my greatest personal development. I recall being the first person I knew to have a 'mobile' phone in the car as I was regularly on the road.

My role included developing new products to meet the needs of new markets, and that brought me in front of leaders of many great businesses in the UK. For example we developed a funding package for customers purchasing a franchise, and developed a branded credit card for an Insurance company. This was a mix of retailing and wholesaling, and quite a lot of entertaining clients. Those were the days we were expected to have an expense sheet!

I spent time in Germany researching their 'Open Plan' bank branches, which was enlightening, and allowed us to be first bank in the UK to open new branches without internal walls or screens. These were viewed as barriers to good customer communication. The German banks also learned that when they moved their ATM's outside, fewer people visited the branches, and business declined. There is a trend in many businesses to automate as much as possible and reduce the HR budget to a minimum. This can be a flawed concept if the business is a B2C model. The strategy of lowering the cost/income ratio is always an admirable trait in a CEO, however, I have learned over the years that increasing revenue, rather than lowering costs best improves this ratio. This and other similar things I learned have informed my work in the Credit Union.

Other than that, I operated my own painting business, a part-time video and photography business, and managed a logistics enterprise for a time. I studied for a Diploma in Accounting and Finance, a Management Diploma, and a Diploma in Lending to the SME sector. And like you, reader, I clocked up many hours of study-time to help with the demands of the job.

During my studies I became amazed at the lack of information specifically aimed at supporting Credit Unions on the subject of strategy. With over three million Credit Union members in this country relying on the strategic choices of managers and CEO's, I felt it is high time that this void was filled. There are a further 214 million members across 57,000 Credit Unions in 105 countries and each in turn has or needs a strategy. If I can reach some of these and help in some way it will be worthwhile.

On the subject of help, I went into Credit Union world about ten years ago, without any real idea of what might be in store for me. The gentleman heading up the lending function at the time was Paddy Reilly, who had served at board level years earlier. Paddy ensured that my transition from the banking and commercial world was a smooth one, and I really appreciated his patience and his support. He had 'been there – done that' and I was the 'newbie'. I remember asking Paddy what a heifer was as I had just met a farming member about a loan! He thought that was funny!

Unfortunately Paddy became ill and later passed away. He fought off cancer as long as he could, and left us with a void that is now filled with fond memories of him and he has a special place in the hearts of many members and staff.

It is unfortunate that cancer continues to affect the lives of so many, and in honour Paddy, I am donating 100% of the sale proceeds of this book to the Irish Cancer Society.

Introduction

First of all thank you for choosing this book and giving consideration to the topic of strategy, which I trust is of interest to you. Strategic thinking is one of the least known or understood management skills. We understand many of the skills that a CEO or manager requires in order to lead a successful business. A manager must be familiar with business continuity management, change management, coaching, communication skills, conflict management, decision-making, delegation, developing team members, leadership, mentoring, motivating or inspiring others, negotiating, performance management, planning, problem-solving, project management, recruitment, and team management, among others; the list is endless.

CEO's and managers work at developing these skills to a reasonable level, but in truth we don't always understand the requirement for a significant capability in the practices of strategic thinking, strategic management and strategic planning.

By the time you have finished this book I hope to have demystified the concept of strategy and placed it in context for you in your Credit Union. It is important to recognise that there are few, if any, experts on the business of strategy and it is in fact a relatively new concept in the world of business.

Until recent years, the word 'strategy' had not been mentioned by anybody in the central bank, at least to Credit Unions, and most likely not to banks either. In 2010 our CEO and board had the foresight to engage external professionals and set about developing a workshop on considering what strategy we should adopt for the future. The strategic planning team consisted of two board members and four of our management. Having spent a few weekends working on the topic it was clear to us that this would be challenging and time-consuming but it would also be of immense value to the board and management, and ultimately to the Credit Union and it's members. Following the amendments to the Credit Union Act in 2012, it is now more appropriate for the management team to be at the forefront of developing draft strategic plans and putting these forward for consideration by the board, rather than have board members formulating the strategy from scratch.

This led us to a suggestion during a Chapter meeting in our city in early 2011, that a representative group of management and board should consider if there might be merit in some form of co-operation amongst the seventeen Credit Unions in the County. These represented 150,000 members and had total assets of €0.75bn. I volunteered to be on the steering group that considered the options for change.

Following several weekends of torturous debate we agreed to present a single proposal to the next Chapter meeting. In July 2011 we proposed that all seventeen Credit Unions merge into ONE Credit Union, with the strongest board in the country. Such a board would have the necessary range of skills to

11

include governance and compliance, financial reporting, HR and training, investment and treasury, marketing and member services, regulatory and audit, communications, credit and credit control, information technology, and legal.

On reflection it was somewhat aspirational to design a board with such a diverse range of skills.

The proposal referred to key risks (financial, operational and external), headline costs, member benefits, and cost savings. Suffice to say the proposal was ahead of its time, and was not well received by the majority of Credit Unions. Many representatives were aghast at the very thought of such a transformation, and were not shy in voicing their dissent. The document was duly filed in various cabinets around the County and never saw the light of day again. Who knows, it may be revisited at some point in the distant future. The fact that I was reading *The Magic of Thinking BIG'* by David J. Schwartz at the time may have over exercised my view on what was possible and what was not!

As is always the case with strategy and strategic thinking, our proposal led to more questions than answers.

The scale of the project and reluctance from others overcame our enthusiasm. Even, perhaps especially, with strategic thinking, timing is everything. If you are searching for a universally agreed definition of strategy, and some brief answers as to how to approach strategy, I apologise in advance, as there are no shortcuts to understanding strategy.

12

Let me put that comment in perspective. Here are some of the questions you and your Credit Union will need to have answers for, or at least attempt to answer in some shape or form. The process of exercising one's cerebral muscles on these and other questions brings about a clearer understanding of your own business and where it is likely to fit in the 'greater scheme of things'.

The BIG Questions

- Who are we?
- What do we do?
- Why are we here?
- What kind of organisation are we?
- What kind of organisation do we want to become?

Questions on Competitiveness and Sustainability

- What is happening in the industry, with our competitors, and in general?
- What are our goals for growth, size, and annual surplus?
- What new products and services will we offer, if any?
- What members or users will we offer them to?
- How will the selling/buying decisions be made?
- What distribution channels will we employ, and are they relative to changing trends?
- What technologies will we use?
- What capabilities and capacities will we require?
- Which capabilities are core?
- Where will we use alliances, joint ventures, co-operation with other suppliers and Credit Unions?
- What are our options?

13

- In which markets will we compete and can we clearly define those market sizes and potential?
- On what basis will we compete?
- Will we be BEST at any aspect of the business?
- What will we NOT get involved in?
- Do we know what our competitive advantage is?
- Are we convinced that it is sustainable?

I hope that as you were reading through this short list, you were thinking of several other profound questions, as this is merely a taster to set the scene! If you raise an eyebrow or scoff at some of the questions, that's fine too. You either have the answers already, or you will find that developing a response to them will be educational and rewarding.

I encourage you to doodle in the book as you read through it. Much of the content will appear abstract at first, and in time will make more sense as you contextualise the information and theories. The fact that you have read to here indicates that you have an open mind, a deep interest in your Credit Union future, and a desire to use whatever tools are available to ensure continued success.

While the following chapters are wide ranging in topics, they are each linked by the golden thread of strategic thinking and strategic actions.

The Context

In May 2015 Ian Guider, the Markets editor of the Sunday Business Post wrote the following:

> 'It was a key date in the diary for the Credit Union registrar, Anne Marie McKiernan. As the chief regulator of the country's hundreds of Credit Unions, McKiernan travelled to Killarney last weekend to the Irish League of Credit Unions (ILCU) annual conference. Her speech was designed to make Credit Unions wake up to some of the problems they faced, but also about the opportunities they had to provide more financial services to their 3.3 million members.
>
> It was also a speech that McKiernan didn't get to deliver, despite her journey to Kerry. Having been due to make the address by mid morning, her time was pushed back until she eventually left without actually speaking, the Sunday Business Post understands.
>
> Instead, a bitter row over the election of a new ILCU president dominated the proceedings.'

The text of her speech would have included:

> 'The critical challenge now for your sector is to address the shortcomings of your business model, your ageing membership base, your ability to grow and develop your product and services offerings and your lending business, and your ability to meet regulatory

15

requirements. As I have commented on publicly before, we have yet to see a sufficiently structured and collaborative response, at the sectoral level, to the scale of business model transformation required to ensure a vibrant future.'

In plain English, this is the regulator pleading with the Credit Union sector to have a coherent strategy to ensure a future for its 3 million members. It's probably fair to say that the sector may not have a clear strategy, and this is partly because each Credit Union is a separate entity with its own board and its own culture (i.e. 'the way things are done around here').

However, each Credit Union does indeed have its own strategy, whether it is in a format acceptable to the powers-that-be or otherwise. This book will help individual Credit Unions to have a deeper understanding of their strategy, and to enhance their capacity to articulate the ingredients that brought about that strategy.

> Strategies need not be deliberate - they can also emerge.

As for the Credit Union movement, the Department of Finance conducted a strategic review of the sector in 2010-2011. The general overview noted; 'This report presents a disturbing risk profile and medium term outlook for the sector.' It subsequently amended the Credit Union Act 1997 which then enforced more regulatory controls and attempts to stabilise the sector.

The areas affected by the amended Act are reserves, liquidity, lending, investments, controls and reporting requirements. This became the Credit Union and Co-Operation with Overseas Regulators Act 2012 (CUCORA).

Clearly the Central Bank has its own strategy and more significantly it is progressing on the most important aspect of any strategy; the execution. It demands that the Credit Union sector in Ireland must have its own coherent strategy, which embraces all the new regulatory guidelines.

It appears that there is a missing link when individual Credit Unions have their own strategy; the regulatory body has a clear strategy on the Credit Union movement, yet the Credit Union movement does not have a unified approach to its own future. That lack of unity does not instill confidence, and presents an opportunity for the Central Bank to subject Credit Unions to firmer enforcement than might otherwise be deemed necessary.

Even when we understand strategy and we develop a deeper appreciation of the need for strategic thinking, it remains the case that strategy is challenging because there are hard choices to be made in deciding what we must do and what not to do. Furthermore, it is not for everyone. There are those who would rather deal with a building on fire than spend a day in the strategic thinking and planning room!

Whatever your disposition, there is no getting away from the necessity to examine your Credit Union's capacity to prosper into the long term. How you do this is up to you, your management team, and your board. How sustainable that future is, will depend on a range of external and internal factors, and on the strength of your commitment to being the master of your own destiny.

On the 7th July 2016 the Irish Times newspaper had the headline 'Shrinking Credit Unions need rethinking' in their 'Business Comment' section. An extract from the article includes:

> 'A €250 million bailout fund set up during the crisis for the sector is only expected to be tapped to the tune of €20 million, as the industry engaged in wholesale restructures and mergers in recent years. But unless there's a serious rethink about where this almost 60-year-old movement is headed, recent efforts may come to naught.'

Reader's notes... ✍

Far and away the best prize that life has to offer
is the chance to work hard at work worth doing.

Theodore Roosevelt

Ask the Experts

Harvard, Cambridge, Stanford, Oxford, Princeton, Yale and Cornell all produce the finest professors of business. Here are some of their often-quoted writers on the subject of strategy. Individuals like Porter and Mintzberg are staple advisors on strategy, planning, competitiveness and change.

Henry Mintzberg

In his 1994 book, *'The Rise and Fall of Strategic Planning'*, he points out that people use 'strategy' in several different ways, the most common being these four:

1) Strategy is a plan; a 'how', a means of getting from here to there.
2) Strategy is a pattern of actions over time.
3) Strategy is position, that is, it reflects decisions to offer particular products or services in particular markets.
4) Strategy is perspective; that is, vision and direction.

Mintzberg argues that strategy **emerges over time** as intentions collide with and accommodate a changing reality. So, one might start with a perspective and decide that it calls for a certain position. It may be agreed that this is to be achieved by way of a carefully crafted plan. These are **intended strategies.**

However, the eventual outcome and strategy will be reflected in a pattern that is evident from decisions and actions taken over time. This pattern in decisions and actions defines what Mintzberg called **emergent strategy**. Emergent strategies can be described as unplanned strategies that arise in response to unexpected opportunities and challenges.

Ultimately, an organisations realised strategy is the product of the intended or deliberate strategy as well as the emergent strategy. Either way the strategy must be realised to be effective.

Michael Porter

In a 1996 *Harvard Business Review* article Porter suggests that competitive strategy is **'about being different'**. He adds, 'It means deliberately choosing a different set of activities to deliver a unique mix of value'. In short, Porter argues that strategy is about competitive position, about differentiating yourself in the eyes of the customer/member, about adding value through a mix of activities **different** from those used by competitors. In his earlier book, Porter defines competitive strategy as 'a combination of the ends (goals) for which the firm is striving and the means (policies) by which it is seeking to get there'. Therefore, Porter seems to embrace strategy as both **plan and position**.

Michel Robert

Michel Robert takes a similar view of strategy in, '*Strategy Pure & Simple*', where he argues that the real issues are **'strategic management' and 'thinking strategically'**. For Robert, this boils down to decisions pertaining to four factors:

- Products and services
- Members/Customers
- Market segments
- Geographic areas

Robert claims that decisions about which products and services to offer, the members to be served, the market segments in which to operate, and the geographic areas of operations should be made on the basis of a single 'driving force'. He claims that ten possible driving forces exist but only one can be the basis for strategy. The ten driving forces cited by Robert are:

— Product or service
— End user members/customers
— Market type
— Production capacity and capability
— Technology
— Sales and marketing method
— Distribution method
— Natural resources
— Size and growth
— Return/Profit/Surplus

Treacy and Wiersema

The notion of restricting the basis on which strategy might be formulated has been carried one step further by Michael Treacy and Fred Wiersema, authors of '*The Discipline of Market Leaders*'. In the *Harvard Business Review* article that presaged their book, Treacy and Wiersema assert that companies achieve leadership positions by narrowing, not broadening, their business focus. Treacy and Wiersema identify **three 'value-disciplines'** that can serve as the basis for strategy: operational excellence; customer intimacy; and product leadership. As with driving forces, only one of these value disciplines can serve as the basis for strategy. Treacy and Wiersema's three value disciplines are briefly defined below:

1. **Operational excellence.** Strategy is predicated on the production and delivery of products and services. The objective is to **lead the industry in terms of price** and convenience. Aldi, Lidl and RyanAir are good examples of operational excellence. This strategy requires a lean cost base.

2. **Product Leadership.** These companies produce a continuous stream of **top of the range products** and services. Pirelli Tyres and Rolex watches are in this space.

3. **Customer Intimacy.** Organisations in this arena work on long term member loyalty and the **best in class service on a personal basis**. For example, Singapore Airlines are renowned for their personal service. Credit Unions fare very well in this category too.

23

Lafley and Martin

In *'Playing to Win'* Lafley and Martin, explain that strategy is more about making truly hard choices, and that winning should be at the heart of any strategy. 'A strategy is a coordinated and integrated set of five choices:

1.   A winning aspiration
2.   Where to play
3.   How to win
4.   Core capabilities, and
5.   Management systems'

Personally I love this book because it simplifies the whole strategy topic and distills it into a sports-like metaphor. It doesn't get any easier than 'where do we want to play, and how do we want to win?' But it is important to note that it is not how to win generally, but how to win within the chosen domains. A few of their recommendations are:

- Do play to win rather than simply to compete.
- Do start with the consumers or members, rather than the products, when thinking about what it means to win.
- Be specific in your choices; if everything is a priority, nothing is.
- A company with a competitive advantage earns a greater margin between revenue and cost than other companies do for engaging in the same activity.
- Be honest about the state of your capabilities.
- Think about clarity and simplicity when communicating key strategic choices to the organisation.

George Steiner

George Steiner, a professor of management and one of the founders of *The California Management Review*, is generally considered a key figure in the origins and development of strategic planning. His book, *'Strategic Planning,'* is close to being a bible on the subject. Yet, Steiner does not bother to define strategy except in the notes at the end of his book. There, he advises that strategy entered into the management literature as a way of referring to what one did to counter a competitor's actual or predicted moves. Steiner also points out in his notes that there is very little agreement as to the meaning of strategy in the business world. Some of the definitions in use to which Steiner pointed include the following:

- Strategy is that which top management does that is of great importance to the organisation.
- Strategy refers to basic directional decisions, that is, to purposes and missions.
- Strategy consists of the important actions necessary to realise these directions.
- Strategy answers the question: What should the organisation (Credit Union) be doing?
- Strategy answers the question: What are the ends we seek and how should we achieve them?

So we can see that even the 'experts' have different views on what strategy is. It is perfectly fine to have an opinion that is contrary to any of the above, or better still to have a view that is a cocktail of these interpretations of strategy. What's most

25

important is that you have an open view as to what strategy is, or might be about.

No matter which definition we rely on, the decisions and choices we make about markets, products, delivery channels, resources, diversification, pricing, and technologies, are the same and invariably as tough.

Reader's notes... ✍

If all the economists were laid end to end,
they'd never reach a conclusion.

George Bernard Shaw

What Good Strategy Looks Like

I am a big fan of describing what something should look like when the job is done. Architects and garden designers take the time to design what the finished job will look and feel like, and the use of CAD (Computer Aided Design) facilitates a 3D concept so all stakeholders have their eyes on the same prize.

A perfect example is the building of the channel tunnel between Dover and Calais. Precision engineering and the sharing of knowledge ensured that the two tunnels met in the middle. There may have been an overspend, but there was no room for error when it came to the main objective of building a 23 mile tunnel under the sea.

You want the very best strategy for your Credit Union. You want a strategy that has a strong chance of success. Your members expect that you will have considered all the variables, taken stock of the current resources in place, that you have looked into the future and observed around you, and prepared a strategic course for your ship that meets the members' expectations.

The Credit Union belongs to all its members. You, whether you are a CEO, or a member, are only 'minding' the Credit Union for the time you are there. You must aim to leave it in a better shape than when you found it. So good strategy will be appropriate to the time and place, and will steer the Credit Union towards success and away from icebergs, storms, obsolescence, and stagnation. Good strategy will always be looking to the future, and will involve all the employees, the board, and key stakeholders.

Here are a few rhetorical questions for when you are close to completing your strategy:

- Do we have individuals who have agreed to be responsible for each of the strategic choices or objectives?

- Will those individuals be capable of managing the execution of those objectives?

- Will our strategy permit us to say that we have a buffer around our business that protects us from substitutes, and new suppliers? Is that buffer considered strong enough to keep the others at bay, or is it possible for others to steal our business from under our noses?

- Do we have a system in our Credit Union where all employees feel connected? At the very least, does everyone feel involved, and that they have an important part to play?

There are several ways to test if your employees are tuned into the correct frequency, but remember, if some are not, it is more than likely your failings rather than theirs. You can often spend hours and hours discussing strategy at management level, and so for you, it is the staple diet of what you do, it's normal; it's part of the conversation. But for some employees, it's a mysterious dialogue that goes on once a week or once a month that they are never part of. It's considered as management's area, like deciding on what local associations or organisations to sponsor, or what interest rates you should charge.

So take time out to test the waters now and again, because you may be presuming too much or too little.

Try this for size! Casually approach a staff member, carrying the current strategic plan document. Leave it down beside the individual and ask, 'Do you know what this is?'

If you get a positive answer you can follow up with something like 'Would you mind explaining it to me? Why do we have it and what are one or two of the key points in it?'

Now this will be daunting to the poor unfortunate individual that you have landed on, so you will need to reassure them as to your purpose. Remember, you are trying to establish how well or otherwise **your** communication is working. One of my mottos is, 'If the message has not been received, it was probably not sent very well'. **You** are responsible for ensuring that the information you send out is received and understood. Simply standing on a platform and announcing some new message at the staff meeting, is no indicator that the message is received, let alone understood.

You should then move to the next level of interaction with your subject and ask, 'Can you explain what you were doing right now and how it helps to contribute to that plan/strategy/goal?'

What you are doing is asking your employee for feedback on the strategy you have for the business. If it's not abundantly clear to them, you have much less chance of realising the component parts of the strategy. You are also gaining a valuable insight into the level of commitment in the organisation, and if that is lacking, you are on a hiding to nothing.

If the latter is true, how will you ever get to a point where you can ask what good strategy looks like? Instead, you are now considering the next question, 'Do employees in this Credit Union know that we have a strategy and that it has some key components that require their input?'

There are several ways to develop the interests of employees and it's best to break the strategy into smaller bite size pieces. So for example, we might start with talking about the following analysis of:

o **The financials**. Have we a comfortable surplus every year or is it increasingly difficult to turn in an acceptable bottom line result?

o **Members needs**. Are we assuming what members want? Have we asked them recently? Which groups of members are likely to borrow more and what channels do we reach them by?

o **Local and national competitors**. What are the local banks and other financial services businesses doing? Who is gaining market share? Which staff members are looking out for these trends and how do they report into the rest of the team? Have we tested the competitors to see what the member experience is like, or are we relying on the anecdotal evidence in the media? Could we be blindsided by a new entrant to the marketplace with a low cost business model?

o **Trends.** Who is using our services and who is not? Do we see business referrals from some staff but not from others? What is working well in other Credit Unions?

o **PESTEL**

- What is going on **Politically** that could have an effect on our business?
- Is the **Economy** improving or stagnant? Is employment on the increase locally, and why? Have we visited the large employers recently and asked them for their view of the next five years?
- Are there **Social** issues that we could do more to help with in the community? Do we have access to individuals on the boards of local community initiatives, and have we assured them that we are here to assist?
- Are there **Technological** developments that will impact the way we do business and are we ready to anticipate that change?
- What are the **Environmental and Legal** issues that concern our members and the employees?

What are the **choices** we have to make about products and

services, distribution channels, staffing and automation, investment, interest rates, member engagement, social dividend, and all the other possible choices that the employees could suggest?

What **actions** will we take now, and what actions will we plan for next year and the year after? Should we change our structure, our operations, our processes, our marketing, or our budget allocations? Whatever we do, we will need to agree sets of objectives and each in turn will have associated actions. This is how we turn aspirations into reality and results.

In short, you check in with the employees to establish common ground for *'where you want to play and how you want to win'*.

When you are happy that your employees are on the same page as the management team and board, you can then ask yourself some of the more difficult questions, for example:

- What is it that we don't know that we need to know, to better understand our business?

- How well are we benefiting from referrals from satisfied members?

- How well do we cater for the needs of the members who are short of time because of life's pressures?

So when you are asking yourself what good strategy looks like, it encompasses a range of involvement and understanding from employees, as well as a clear and coherent proposition for member service.

Great strategy will ensure the future of the Credit Union, provide sustainable growth through a deep knowledge of members' needs and members' choices, and match the resources needed to deliver the goods.

Let us also be clear that great strategy identifies the individuals who are unwilling or incapable of participating in building the future of the Credit Union, and provides those individuals with an alternative career path. These are the tough choices that need to be made for the good of the Credit Union as a whole.

Reader's notes... ✍

All labour that uplifts humanity has dignity and importance and should be undertaken with painstaking excellence.

Martin Luther King, Jr.

Design Thinking, a Brief Insight

Steve Jobs put it well when he said:

> 'Most people make the mistake of thinking design is what it looks like. People think it's this veneer — that the designers are handed this box and told, 'Make it look good!' That's not what we think design is. It's not just what it looks like and feels like. **Design is how it works.**'

In this section I want to briefly cover the concept of Design Thinking as a process for facilitating strategy and innovation.

When we see a great idea introduced, we often say to ourselves 'Why didn't I think of that?' It's as if someone had a brainwave and out popped the concept, fully formed. The reality is that significant resources will have been applied over a lengthy timeframe, along with inspiration, innovation, perspiration and motivation.

'Marketing is making people want things.

Design Thinking is making things people want'

Design Thinking is more about **looking for options** than looking for answers, and this is a difficult concept to come to terms with at first. Most of us have trained our thinking to look for answers, as we need to make decisions quickly every day, based on any given set of circumstances. We see a problem and we look for the solution, then we fix the problem. It's generally that simple, in theory anyway! It gets a little more difficult when we add reality, emotions, and individual human reactions into the mix.

Design Thinking looks firstly at the existing product or service that doesn't fully meet the changing needs of the consumer, or discovers a 'need' that is not being met. For Credit Unions it involves a perspective of really getting into the shoes of the member, and feeling first hand what the experience is like for that member or group of members. This is called **empathy** and begins to let you **understand the consumer** and the market.

Gifted design thinkers focus on the small details, which others may not reflect on. Some people refer to this as the customer journey, and magnify each part of the journey to see what is annoying, outdated, frustrating, repetitive, time-consuming, and so on. They **observe** the audience and begin to **define** the 'pain' or 'inconvenience' or 'time waster'. This leads to looking at alternatives, and by standing in the shoes of our members we can challenge the status quo. Using those famous two words of George Bernard Shaw, and 'borrowed' by JFK, design thinkers ask 'Why not?'

> The difference between an idea and a concept is like the difference between a list of ingredients and a recipe.

Instead of reaching for the sticking plaster, design thinkers facilitate the process of **idea generation** through brainstorming, peer discussions, cross company innovation groups, and encouraging input from many disciplines (e.g. engineering, sales, technology, strategists). In a Credit Union, this could be facilitated by drawing from marketing, credit control, lending, member services, financial control, and of course the added dimension of members input.

After the idea generation phase, creative solutions are offered for consideration and one or more **prototype** offerings are developed. At this stage it is best to maintain an open mind towards your colleague's suggestions and proposals as you need to develop an innovative culture if one does not already exist.

These prototypes are then **tested** internally and with user groups so as to check the **added value and benefits**, and how the members perceive them. This is part of the **delivery** phase, and ultimately the Credit Union must deliver value to the member while **capturing value** in the form of additional revenue or cost saving.

A simple chart below depicts the process.

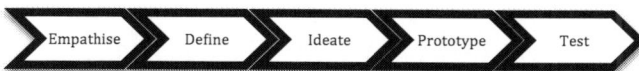

Empathise → Define → Ideate → Prototype → Test

You may be one of those individuals who believes that your capacity to think clearly and quickly is one of your best attributes and this design thinking is for someone else. You may be right! However, consider for a moment how this approach might bring out some innovative thinking from your management team, your board, or your staff.

Would they tend to be more receptive to change and perhaps be the instigators of change, rather than have you pulling teeth every time you need to look at something through a different lens? There may be merit in using design thinking as a tool to develop others if you don't need developing in this capacity yourself. If it helps to produce what your members want, then it has to go into your toolbox. You can choose to use it for diversity, or simply to maintain the element of surprise with your work colleagues.

I once heard that creativity is referred to as **risky** at the beginning, and lauded as **innovative** when it's successful. So it's perfectly fine to feel like you and your team have lost your marbles during the early stages of creativity and innovation. This is to be expected and don't be tempted to abandon the process. You will only be thanked when the results literally pay dividends.

Below are some attributes of a creative team. Choose one or two at a time to focus on bringing into your team.

✓ Trust and openness

✓ Debates and clashes of viewpoints

✓ Freedom of expression

✓ Playfulness/humour

✓ Conflict management

✓ Encouraging risk taking

✓ Support for new ideas

39

✓ Idea wall or time wall

✓ Being comfortable with creativity

✓ Creativity that adds value

✓ Dynamism and liveliness

When you are trying to make the best use of the available resources as a leader, it is incumbent on you to find different ways to tap into the innovative and creative minds of those around you.

There are four questions that you should ask yourself, or ask of your team. Your managers should check these with their staff.

1) **If you were competing against our business, what would you do?** This involves taking a few steps back from the business and looking at the Credit Union through the eyes of members. Your teams will doubtless suggest some great ideas and identify some gaps that need to be plugged.

2) **What is currently impossible to do that, if it were possible, would change everything?** This is the opportunity for the innovative and creative employees to have their say. Everything goes on the table, and all suggestions are considered. When an employee suggests a game changer it is time to listen up.

3) **What are you trying to make happen in the next three months?** A question of this nature focuses the mind on results. What goal is in your mind that will make this Credit

Union different at the end of ninety days? Perhaps some individuals are working on a project that you had no idea about and this allows for some airtime and recognition.

4) **If nothing changes, what is likely to happen?** A question like this one will test the employee understanding of the changing environment. Because there may have been little or no change for a long time, they may have presumed that no change is required in the future. The answer to this question could be an eye opener for senior management. It's also a huge question to ask of board members.

Reader's notes... ✍

Don't judge each day by the harvest you reap
but by the seeds that you plant.

Robert Louis Stevenson

When the Dividend was the Only Strategy

'If I have seen further, it is by standing upon the shoulders of giants'. This is the quote made famous by Sir Isaac Newton in a letter written to a fellow scientist Robert Hooke in February 1675.

The phrase is understood to mean that if Newton had been able to discover more about the universe than others, then it was because he was working in the light of discoveries made by fellow scientists, either in his own time or earlier.

So it is for most of us who are privileged to work in a Credit Union today. We would not be in successful Credit Unions and working on strategic plans, were it not for the unstoppable energies and commitment of those who preceded us.

Each decade presents fresh challenges to those volunteers and employees charged with developing a Credit Union.

Until about ten years ago, the decision that attracted most controversy was probably about how much to distribute as annual dividend on savings. This was valued as a key indicator of success, and clearly it worked to a large extent. Boards would reflect on what was paid the previous years and see if

43

they could pay a similar dividend or perhaps even improve on it.

At the time it was an essential part of building trust and building sizeable cash deposits. It was not possible for a Credit Union to grow if the members were reluctant to deposit their savings and allow the Credit Union to lend it out in small chunks.

The financial crash in 2007 saw banks worldwide running for cover. In our own country, we discovered over time that every rule in the book was interpreted in whatever way suited the occasion. The lack of good governance and oversight contributed to poor decision-making and many years later the country is still paying the price.

> Ultimately the PURPOSE of strategy is to guarantee the future cash flow of the business.

This has brought about considerable change in the regulatory framework. And of course it was met with some resistance.

I recall being at the AGM of our representative body and listening to a Credit Union board director making the statement:

> 'If this financial regulator thinks he can lead us around the field like we were a bull with a ring in our nose, he has another thing coming. Who does he think he is?'

This degree of resistance to change was expected, because at the time, several banks had failed and were in state ownership, but Credit Unions, whilst appearing to be less professional, had not caused any damage and had not failed or put its members funds at risk.

With the changes came the need to bolster reserves, and change the thinking on how much was distributed back to savers, in tandem with the decision to strengthen the balance sheet.

At the time most balance sheet reserves were in single percentage figures, and today it is rare to see a Credit Union with less than 10% reserves. That is a significant development across all Credit Unions during a time when bad and doubtful debts were being provided for at an unprecedented rate. It is a tribute to Credit Unions that members continued to increase their savings while the big 'cleanup' was in progress. Many commentators feared the exodus of savings from Credit Unions where their Annual General Meetings were postponed or delayed for accounting or other regulatory reasons. But members not only left their savings in situ, they continued to save at an increasing rate.

Whilst this is to be lauded, strategy is less about the dividend and more concerns the long-term viability of the business. Some Credit Unions contract out their strategic plan to a third party, whilst others persevere and perspire over the contents. Either way, it behooves each individual Credit Union to examine its resources and capabilities, and develop strategies that ensures it remains relevant to its members.

For some, if that means paying a dividend as well as offering the latest financial management tools, then so be it. For others it will mean that they can offer the best priced loans in the neighbourhood, and if that works for them, that's fine too.

Still other Credit Unions will differentiate themselves on the member experience and the value proposition, and they will need to outline this in a coherent fashion in their strategic plan and as far as possible show that the plan is bullet proof in the face of competition and changing circumstances. I will spend a little time looking at the value proposition in a later chapter.

Reader's notes... ✍

Someone is sitting in the shade today
because someone planted a tree a long time ago.

Warren Buffett

Questions to Ponder about your Credit Union

When I met Bernard Marr, the author of *Strategic Performance Management* and other publications, he spoke about an interesting concept he developed called 'Key Performance Questions'. He suggests that 'If you ever feel that you are collecting a lot of seemingly meaningless information in your organisation, then just ask the question 'What is the Key Performance Question we are trying to answer with this data?'

The purpose of this section is to prompt you to ask more challenging questions of the business, the operations, the strategy you adopt, and the supports and resources you rely on to execute that strategy.

For example what is the strategy of your competitors? If it's the same as yours, then you may have a strategy but you don't have a smart one. Is it possible or evident that most of your competitors made the same choice as your Credit Union?

Do you spend the beginning of each month analysing the previous month and comparing it to past performance, and the budgeted figures for the month? You submit quarterly prudential returns to the Central Bank, and in turn analyse the data on a quarterly basis, and in some instances compare to your peers, and the national picture.

48

Bernard Marr recommends that we look at each of the strategic objectives in our strategic plan, and design a Key Performance Question (or two or three) for each objective. They should be open questions, and looking to the present and the future, not the past. An example of such a question could be, 'Are we increasing our market share?'

Another few examples are:

- To what extent are we responding to the most exciting opportunities that the market is offering?

- How well are we meeting the needs of our members who are at college, or those who joined us in the past three months?

- In what ways are we enhancing our reputation with peer Credit Unions and key stakeholders?

- What is the population of our Common Bond, and how many of them hold an account and/or borrow?

- How much business is available if we managed to serve everyone in our common bond?

- How many of our members are borrowing in the bank, from moneylenders, on the Internet, or peer-to-peer?

Ask how do you hire new people? Is it through your own network, or do you go to the marketplace and identify the best people with the appropriate talents, skills, experience and attitude? Many business owners have discovered that hiring people from your personal network will fill the gap, but it is not the optimal solution. Occasionally the individual you hire from your personal network will be as good or better than you can find anywhere, but this is the exception rather than the rule.

Do you take the easy route and give all employees the same pay rise each year, or the same bonus? This may be the easiest option but it has the effect of satisfying the under-performers and frustrating the over-performers. If employees exceed expectations in their roles, they expect recognition and reward, and the annual pay rise or bonus is the ideal opportunity to facilitate this expectation. In fact if you reward an under-performer you will most likely be the direct cause of continued under performance. This is an area of the business strategy that most organisations are uncomfortable with. If you feel the same way you are in good company. Nonetheless, your employees who excel must be rewarded in a manner that does not mirror your under performers, and this will require some bold decisions on your part.

Have you given any of the employees an increased level of responsibility or promotion in the hope that they will start to perform as they should perform? There is no shortage of research to indicate that when you promote a non-performer, employees tend to respond by reducing their outputs. It can often be tempting to give an employee a bump up the responsibility ladder because you recognise their potential. However, the current performance must at least be up to a required standard, before you can start wishful thinking about their potential. That begs the question; 'Do all employees know the agreed standards for technical expertise and for behaviours?'

Traditionally we are comfortable with questioning trends, volumes, margins, comparisons, and so on. These are no more than the results of the bigger questions, which we usually shy away from. That's because some questions are outside our comfort zone and are much more difficult to grapple with.

Think for a moment if you ask your next management meeting, 'How satisfied are the last 500 members who borrowed and what could we do to improve the experience of the next 500?' Or, 'Which parts of our marketing spend are giving us the best returns, and where should we spend less/more?' Would there be an awkward silence or do you and your team have such a grip on the business that you could at least attempt to respond to that type of question? Challenge your team to ask similar questions.

You can then encourage your chairperson to reflect on the last few thought-provoking questions from the boardroom. Which board members never challenge the figures, the results, or a proposed strategy? And which board members add value to the meetings regularly? Conversely, what has your Credit Union chairperson done to develop individuals and promote an air of participation? There is an abundance of help available in this respect once the issue is recognised as worth improving.

How does your board define a successful meeting? Is it one that finishes early, or where you get through all the agenda items? What does a successful board meeting look like and is this a view shared by all board members?

Does your board spend about 20% of the time looking at the financial results (i.e. looking in the rear view mirror) and 80% of the time looking forward and agreeing business strategy? Current thinking suggests that this 80/20 ratio is about right for a progressive board meeting. You have to ask if there is any benefit in spending an entire board meeting looking in the rear view mirror, yet some boards can fall into this trap without recognising it.

Finally, have your employees been given permission to voice awkward questions, or concerns? If the staff are not asking difficult questions now and again, it may be because they fear reprisals, or they simply are not connected into the cogs of the wheels that drive the business forward. The concerns of one employee are as important as the next internal audit or consultants report. Once this view is understood and there is a culture of welcoming difficult questions from employees, you will find that most problems do not have time to develop any roots and they can be addressed early.

If you find that while reading through some of these questions you recognise an issue you intended to address, just make a mark beside the item. You can identify a suitable 'champion' in the Credit Union to research this and bring forward proposals to implement it. Sometimes an idea needs an individual attached to it in order for it to develop legs.

Reader's notes... ✍

Before I refuse to take your questions,
I have an opening statement.

Ronald Regan

Are you Competing against Other Credit Unions?

From listening to comments over the years I would say that about 80% of the general public believe that all Credit Unions are connected and are part of the same organisation. Much of the media is of a similar view, and who could blame them?

We share the same logo, the same ethos, the same forms and services, and a similar way of doing business with members.

Those of us who are inside the Credit Union movement recognise that no two Credit Unions are the same. We understand that each has its own corporate structure and more importantly each has developed its individual culture and personality over many years.

Credit Unions offer loan interest rates at 2%, 3%, and every rate up to 12%, which is the maximum allowed under the Credit Union Act in Ireland. When I chat to the different CEOs to probe the 'strategy' behind the different interest rates, each will have their own logic, and afirm belief that their thinking is correct. I have met other CEOs who charge a single rate of 12% for all loans and loan classes and are fully convinced that their business model supports that rate.

This is not a criticism of any individual Credit Union, as decisions on rates are based on many circumstances. Indeed it is very possible that each is correct for its own particular set of circumstances and status.

That said, it is certainly a challenge when a member quotes one or two other Credit Unions who offer better loan rates than your Credit Union. As you attempt to explain your position to the member you will no doubt make reference to the benefits of dealing with your Credit Union and why so many other members choose you first.

Most of this goes over the heads of members because they simply can't see why two organisations that are 'the same' can be so 'different'! Little does the average member know that there are significant drivers pushing rates up or down, which are of greater or lesser importance in different Credit Unions.

This brings us to the core difference between Credit Unions and other financial services providers in the community. If we were to define the single most important differentiator it is the presence of friendly, professional **people** serving **members**, not customers.

When we are doing our job as well as we should we will have an unbreakable bond with each of our members. They should be lauding the member experience to their friends and family. They should have little regard for whether the loan interest rate is more or less in a neighbouring Credit Union. They belong to a unique 'club' that was set up by their community and for several decades was run on a voluntary basis by people in the community. Their 'club' has a board of volunteers from the same community.

These sentiments should be front-of-mind. If we allow our members to get caught up on the price, and only the price, we have failed miserably. Indeed if we have put price so high on the list of attributes or priorities, we have caused our own failure. Credit Unions were never intended to be the cheapest, but we should always be the best.

In a world where products and services are often homogenised, it leaves the gate open for Credit Unions to offer an outstanding personal service at a fair price. We are not selling cheese, or socks, or pens. NO, we are providing members with access to some of the brightest, enthusiastic, professionally educated staff in the community. These staff are there to listen, support, advise and help. Our employees show empathy, and are always conscious that the member employs us to look after their best interests. This service is simply not available elsewhere. Having worked in a high street bank for twenty years, I can categorically confirm that there is a different philosophy in the banking world. It can often be just as pleasant and personal. However, the bottom line in the banking sector is earnings per share and that strongly impacts on the underlying motive behind those pleasant and personal smiles.

If your Credit Union can provide that class of outstanding service on a consistent basis, you can afford to let a few members migrate to another Credit Union now and again to avail of cut-price deals.

There are three rules for business. They are framed over my desk and I unashamedly recommend them to you.

RULE 1	RULE 2	RULE 3
BETTER BEFORE CHEAPER	REVENUE BEFORE COST	THERE ARE NO OTHER RULES

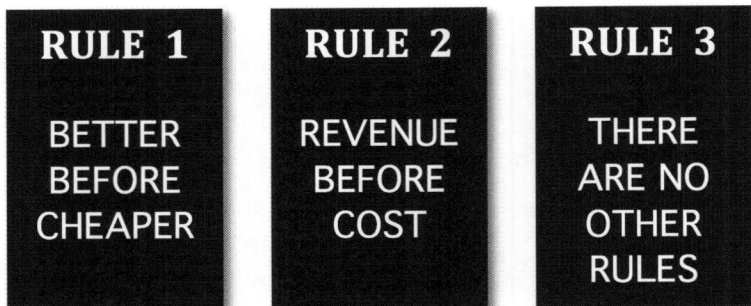

I found these rules in an article in the March 2013 edition of Harvard Business Review. It's called the *3 Rules for Success*. You can locate this nine-paged article online or at your library. It's a fascinating statistical study of 25,453 companies over 44 years. Several hundred were identified as being good enough for long enough to qualify as truly exceptional. It revealed that their strategic choices over decades of success have been consistent with three elementary rules.

These three rules go to the very heart of your business model, and you can agree or disagree with them, but either way you need to decide if you are planning to be **cheaper or better**. The world is full of businesses that were the cheapest option and many of those businesses eventually fail, for several reasons.

You are probably more familiar with those businesses who are renowned for offering the **best** service or product, and for some reason they seem to stand the test of time more often than not. I will address the member value proposition shortly, then look more closely at the topic of price.

57

So, to recap on the issue of competition from local Credit Unions, you have a few choices:

1. Match or beat their interest rates;

2. Merge with them & eliminate the competitive issue; or

3. Offer a better service so your members return to do business with you time and time again.

Can you offer a better service? Of course you can. Every Credit Union and every business has the capacity to offer a better service, a more personal service, and be more relevant to the community it serves.

The magic is being able to do this on a **consistent** basis, with the optimum level of resources.

Reader's notes...

Any idiot can face a crisis —
it's day-to-day living that wears you out.

Anton Chekhov

Mission, Vision and Values

Lets take a look at those three divine mysteries; mission, vision and values. Most of us have a fair idea of what a value is and we have different views on what a mission and a vision should look like.

In this chapter I will explain what the differences are and how we can have a conversation where everyone understands the same principles.

The Mission

Your Credit Union **MISSION** is all about the goals and refers to the over-riding purpose of the Credit Union. The best way to understand your mission is to ask the question:

'What business are we in?'

Answering that question will guide board and management to focus on what is central to the strategy of the business.

Mission
Statement

'What
Business are
we in?'

The mission statement will provide clarity to the employees, board, and indeed to the members about what the Credit Union is fundamentally there to do.

To help in formulating the mission statement, we ask ourselves what difference we make to individuals, and to the community we serve.

Are we there to provide access to finance? To support local initiatives? To improve peoples lives? To help solve problems? To offer an alternative to moneylenders and finance houses? Sometimes the answer to 'Why are we here' is found by asking individual members the question directly. You may think you know why your Credit Union exists, but can members add another dimension to that answer? Their responses will vary from location to location and across different Credit Unions.

The best mission statements are: **Clear, Memorable, and Concise.**

About fifteen or twenty words will suffice, and preferably less. Here are some examples of mission statements for well-known organisations:

- ASSURANT: To be the premier provider of targeted specialised insurance products and related services in North America and selected other markets.

- FORD MOTOR CO: We are a global family with a proud heritage passionately committed to providing personal mobility for people around the world.

- LEVI STRAUSS & Co: People love our clothes and trust our company. We will market the most appealing and widely worn casual clothing in the world. We will clothe the world.

- NIKE Inc: To bring inspiration and innovation to every

61

athlete in the world.

- OXFAM: To create lasting solutions to poverty, hunger and social injustice.

- STARBUCKS: To inspire and nurture the human spirit – one person, one cup and one neighbourhood at a time.

You may think some of these are too short or some too long. Below is one of the longer mission statements, Walt Disney:

'The Walt Disney Company's objective is to be one of the world's leading producers and providers of entertainment and information, using its portfolio of brands to differentiate its content, services and consumer products.'

Personally I believe it lacks character and inspiration, given the audience and the customers of Disney. It may be written in a way to appeal to the corporate investors who need to be assured about the 'portfolio of brands'. And, in fairness to Disney, Credit Unions operate in a different space, as we are not-for-profit organisations.

Wouldn't it be great to know that each board member and every employee in your Credit Union knew the mission statement? If that is an aspiration then you need to consider **brevity, clarity and impact**. The challenge for your Credit Union is to take all views into account and produce a succinct mission statement that members understand and will resonate with them. Something to give them a feeling of safety and security when they read it or hear it. And something that employees smile about when they proudly say the words.

You could consider brainstorming ideas for your mission statement. Bring a selection of your team together and get as many ideas and concepts onto the flipchart without comment or analysis. Keep the process as creative as possible in order to fuel the flow of ideas from the group. When you have exhausted the supply of comments and ideas, you can begin the task of eliminating any duplication and prioritising those concepts that have the greatest appeal. This process will sometimes identify the key phrase or words that form the basis of your mission statement.

Reader's notes...

The Vision

Lets look at the **VISION**, or the vision statement. You are taking into account the current status of the Credit Union, and looking to the future, and aspiring to create something greater than what you have right now. This is different to stating why you exist, which is more factual. The vision is asking the question 'If we are all here in ten years time what will we have created, and what will we have achieved?' This is a stretching aspiration and says, **'If we get everything right, this is what it will look like'.**

Every great leader has a vision for the future. Many great employees have a vision for their own future and the future of the organisation they work for. It is the vision that harnesses the energies and the passions of the people in the Credit Union. A common objective, so to speak. It provides a shared purpose over and above the usual targets and objectives. When you hear members describe the Credit Union with pride, they are not mentioning the dividend, the interest rate, or the size of the reserves. They will point to the help they got in times of need, and the empathy from the people within the Credit Union.

> Vision Statement
>
> 'What sort of future do we want to create?'

The vision statement could be described as the **anchor point of a strategic plan,** as it acts as a funnel to direct the efforts of individuals, teams, and stakeholders. As the adage goes, 'we are all singing off the same hymn-sheet'.

Let's look at some guidelines to creating a good vision statement:

- Keep it short and punchy. Ideally one sentence, and no more than two.

- It should be specific to your Credit Union business and provide a unique outcome that only you can provide.

- Make sure that it is ambitious enough to add some excitement, yet absolutely possible given all the right circumstances and commitment. Bold, but not outlandish.

- It must be in plain English so that members or a new employee understand it when read once. So no jargon or technological speak.

- It will be aligned to the behaviours you want your employees to exhibit in the course of their daily interaction with members and the community generally.

Another way of looking at a vision statement is to include the following aspects in the statement:

- What is it about our Credit Union that is different to other suppliers of financial services?

- We take in deposits and lend that same money out at a margin, but what is the outcome of those actions for the members?

- Most businesses exist to meet the needs of people, so include that need in your statement.

- Measure the level of community reach you aspire to. Are you looking to serve every living soul in your community, or the ones who become members, or is there another measurement?

There are many great examples of vision statements that inspire the company employees and give them a clear path to a shared success. Here are five of them:

- IKEA: To create a better everyday life for the many people.

- MICROSOFT: A computer on every desk and in every home, all running Microsoft software.

- ROYAL BANK OF SCOTLAND: The best bank to work for, the best bank to bank with, the best bank to invest in.

- TOYOTA: To achieve long-term, stable growth in harmony with the environment, the global economy, the local communities it serves, and its stakeholders.

- VODAFONE: To be the communications leader in an increasingly connected world.

Perhaps the best example of a clear vision is the J F Kennedy speech at the joint sessions of Congress on 25th May 1961, and he said, 'I believe that this nation should commit itself to achieving the goal, before this decade is out, of landing a man on the moon and returning him safely to the earth.'

This speech had:

- an ambitious aspiration or goal,
- a defined timeframe,
- a who,
- a what,
- a how, and
- a desired result.

To my mind it is the perfect vision statement. It asks for a commitment to rally behind the almost impossible, but somehow achievable objective.

The strategic plan without a shared vision is nothing other than a 'list of jobs'.

You may get by with just some of your board and employees having an understanding of your **mission**, or why you exist, (though I don't advise it) but you certainly need every single stakeholder to see your Credit Union **vision** as clearly as you see it. You need to articulate it so often that it becomes repetitive and embedded in the conversations. You can't expect employees, management and board to be fully supportive of a plan for the sake of the plan. But if the strategic plan is aligned into the Credit Union shared vision, you have the makings of a team pulling together in one direction, and that is half the job done.

The Five Whys

Perhaps you are struggling to identify or create a vision for your Credit Union. Consider using the **five whys** approach. Start with a descriptive statement of what you do, and by the time you have asked 'why?' five times you will be getting down to the fundamental purpose of your Credit Union. This system is a seasoned approach to getting a deep understanding of the organisation's purpose. You don't need to tell your team that you are practicing your five whys but you will find the opportunity over time to drill down this way.

After asking yourself the five whys, approach your team and board for their opinion of your result. Or set it as a group task during a board meeting.

Reader's notes... ✍

The Values

I find that **VALUES** are more readily understood than mission or vision, as they are more clear-cut. These should be similar or possibly identical to the values the Credit Union founders ascribed to. Those same values should not erode over time, and should be strong enough to face changing technologies, economic cycles, and the variety of management styles that will come and go over the years.

A statement of your Credit Union values will communicate the enduring **core principles** that guide your Credit Union's strategy, and it will offer guidance on how the organisation should operate. Try to ensure that stated values are non confrontational.

L.L.Bean is a shoe manufacturer in the USA and has had the same core value statement since the 1920's, which is to: 'Sell good merchandise at a reasonable profit, treat our customers like human beings, and they will always come back for more.'

> Core Values guide the employee's behaviour, attitude, language, and focus.

This type of value statement becomes a way of life and a way of conducting business, and it is unlikely to change in the next fifty years. Its simplicity has a certain appeal.

Core values can help employees to know the company culture, to discern what is right from wrong, and this can help a business to know if it is on the right path to fulfill its business

69

goals. Apple Inc., for example has a core value of innovation and excellence and this is embodied in their 'Think Differently' motto.

There are many types of core values and you need to understand the ones that are right and fitting for your Credit Union. Some examples of core values are:

- Honest
- Dependable
- Reliable
- Respectful
- Community focused
- Professional
- Personable
- Efficient
- Confidential
- Trustworthy
- Safety
- Helpful

So, lets take a look at four examples from around the corporate world. Many companies have decided to simply list their core values in an image or a display, rather than construct sentences or paragraphs.

1. Takeda

Takeda.ie is the Irish subsidiary of Japan's no. 1 pharmaceutical company, and one of the world's top 100 companies. They have an excellent way of displaying what is important to them as shown in the diagram below.

We can see that **teamwork, commitment, transparency, innovation, passion and diversity** are six core values. However they are telling their employees, board and all stakeholders that **fairness, honesty and perseverance** are even more important core values.

And in the centre of the diagram we can see that **integrity** is their most important core value. So we can begin to understand something about this company by the weighting they place on different values.

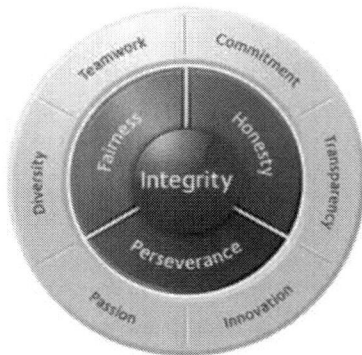

2. Accenture

'High Performance Delivered' is the tagline for this global professional services company. They list six core values:

- Stewardship
- The best people
- Client value creation
- One global network
- Respect for the individual
- Integrity

These are familiar values, and ones that a Credit Union might relate to.

3. Google

On the other hand when we look at the Google values they look like this:

- Focus on the user and all else will follow
- It's best to do one thing really, really well
- Fast is better than slow
- Democracy on the web works
- You don't need to be at your desk to need an answer
- You can make money without doing evil
- There's always more information out there
- The need for information crosses all borders
- You can be serious without a suit
- Great just isn't good enough

As you can see, there is a strong link between the culture of an organisation and the stated core values.

4. IKEA

Many of us have had the unique experience that is shopping in IKEA, but it's unlikely that you will have any idea of their core values. These are what IKEA state to be their core values:

- Humbleness and willpower
- Leadership by example
- Daring to be different
- Togetherness and enthusiasm
- Cost-consciousness
- Constant desire for renewal
- Accept and delegate responsibility

The first thing we notice here is the pairing of values, and this allows for a short list but a higher number of values. The second interesting feature is that they are front and centre with their cost management value, and not ashamed to shout it out.

In summary, the decision to take core values seriously is an important one, as they set the foundation for the organisation culture and for certain behaviours. They will be the reason some people join your Credit Union as employees or as members, and the reason others may leave.

Most of all, your Credit Union's core values will determine how you serve your members and how others perceive you.

73

That is what it's all about. Or as one CEO put it: 'The members come first or they don't come at all'.

Reader's notes... ✍

Change your opinions, keep to your principles;
change your leaves, keep intact your roots.

Victor Hugo

Strategic Leadership

I'm sure that you have read many definitions of leadership and most likely you have your own view of what defines good leadership. Managing and leading may seem similar but fill different roles.

Harvard's John Kotter argues that **good management** is about bringing order and consistency to the **operational aspects** of organisations, such as quality and profitability of products and services. In contrast to good management, **good leadership** is about **coping with change**. Strategic change is therefore central to your ability to apply effective leadership.

In other words, if there were to be no change experienced, a Credit Union would not have any need for a great leader or CEO. Good managers would be sufficient. However every CEO aspires to succeed beyond just keeping the Credit Union ticking over!

Strategic leadership is about starting **uncomfortable conversations** before someone else does. You know you are on the right track if you can recall some of the most uncomfortable conversations you started in the past six months. If you haven't started any difficult dialogue, it's likely that someone else is mulling over the serious issues and you are avoiding them.

What are the biggest and most radical thoughts that you and your team had in recent months? Have you been going through the motions with the usual agenda, or have you been tackling the burning issues and addressing difficult challenges? You might like to ask of any one of your management team what they thought was a big issue; one that was identified, examined and actioned. The same question can be asked of any of the board members. A blank look or stunned silence will tell you enough about how self-challenging your team is. A dynamic team in a high performance culture will not display blank looks.

Another way of looking at this is to consider whether we actively probe and go looking for trouble or do we wait until it arrives? Better to go and confront the issues before they confront your Credit Union. As the motto goes, attack is often the best form of defence. This has been applied to many fields of endeavour, including games and military combat. Also known as the **Strategic Offensive** principle of war. In a nutshell, the idea is that proactivity instead of a passive attitude will preoccupy the opposition and ultimately hinder its ability to mount an opposing counter-attack, leading to a strategic advantage. This way you and your Credit Union are prepared for the future.

Many organisations now look for the skill of **foresight** in a potential CEO. It is expected that every board member and managers at all levels will have ample **insight**. That is to say they have a sound knowledge of the external environment, as well as a strong grasp of the internal dynamics of the organisation.

77

Foresight is considered much more useful to a business. It is the ability to see trends, and particularly to see or predict future trends. There should be no surprises for the CEO of a Credit Union. In theory you should be able to see into the future and have enough gut feeling that you can see trouble or opportunity coming around the corner.

The advantage in seeing trends before your competitors is obvious. You have the time to rationally think through your strategy for dealing with the issue and either extract the maximum benefit, or minimise the damage. These are the opportunities and threats you identify in your SWOT (Strengths, Weaknesses, Opportunities, Threats) analysis.

Some of the best leaders are blessed with fantastic radar. They don't just see around corners, they actively look around corners to see if there is anything lurking in the darkness. They see beyond the hills and into the distance. Over the years, this skill is honed so that it becomes second nature to sniff out opportunities and threats while they are still a distance away. It's a skill worth practicing until it is second nature. Some of us can smell the toast burning before it starts to smoke, and others see the smoke and then realise that there is something not quite right. These senses can be improved with practice and often out of necessity.

To elaborate, an event is something that happens once. Several events may be a pattern, and your challenge is to link the events in order to establish if there is a pattern. This is the benefit of a finely tuned functional personal radar.

As this chapter is on strategic leadership, let me mention that there are eight core beliefs of extraordinary leaders. Geoffrey James, contributing editor to Inc.com, interviewed several of the most successful CEO's in the world to discover their management secrets. The best of the best tended to display the following core beliefs:

1. **Business is an ecosystem**, not a battlefield. Extraordinary leaders naturally create teams that adapt easily to new markets and opportunities. They understand Darwin's Law that looks to the ability to adapt in order to survive and thrive.

2. A company is a community, not a machine. Extraordinary leaders **inspire employees** to dedicate themselves to the success of their peers, and therefore to the community – the Credit Union.

3. **Management is service**, not control. Great leaders set a general direction, and then set about obtaining the resources that their employees need to get the job done. They allow teams and individuals to form their own rules by encouraging decision making at lower levels.

4. **Employees are my peers**, not my children. Extraordinary bosses treat each individual as if they were the only employee in the company. Excellence is expected in all corners and at every level. Consequently, employees take responsibility for their own destinies.

5. **Motivation comes from vision**, not from fear.

Extraordinary bosses inspire people to see a better future and how they will be a part of it. As a result, employees work harder because they believe in the organisation's goals, truly enjoy what they're doing and know they'll share in the rewards.

6. **Change equals growth**, not pain. Extraordinary bosses see change as an inevitable part of life. While they don't value change for its own sake, they know that success is only possible if both employees and organisation embrace new ideas and new ways of doing business.

7. **Technology offers empowerment**, not automation. Extraordinary bosses see technology as a way to free up human beings to be creative and to build better relationships. They adapt their back-office systems to the tools, like smartphones and tablets, which people actually want to use.

8. **Work should be fun**, not mere toil. Extraordinary bosses see work as something that should be inherently enjoyable — and believe therefore that the most important job of a manager is, as far as possible, to put people in jobs that can and will make them truly contented.

As leaders we can claim to cause results but often we fail to recognise that these results are 95% due to the efforts of so many predecessors and of current colleagues. How would it be possible to have a super month of loan growth or upgrade one of our branches if it were not for the efforts of volunteers and staff in the past years? We may not have a Credit Union without all those days, nights and hours of effort by the great people who were here at the start and long before we arrived to take over the reins.

Furthermore, when we successfully launch a new product or when we receive recognition for service excellence, let us not discount the efforts of those predecessors who built the business from scratch.

None of us can achieve on our own. We need our colleagues to watch our backs, to maintain the mundane while we fly the flag, and to offer that smile and greeting to each precious member while we wade through the swamp of strategy and planning.

In recognising this we should acknowledge and appreciate all our colleagues as often as possible and maintain **open communication**. Keep the language plain but not simplistic. Employees recognise the signs when you are merely going through the motions. You have to show up physically and emotionally as a leader to generate the sense of relationship.

I have a preferred author on the topic of strategy. Jim Collins, who has sold millions of books and produced volumes of empirical research, is respected by academics and professional alike.

He uses the term **'Level 5 leaders'** to describe individuals who channel their ego needs away from themselves and into the larger goal of building a great company. It's not that Level

81

5 leaders have no ego or self-interest. Indeed they are incredibly ambitious, but their ambition is first and foremost for the institution, not for themselves.

The levels are outlined as follows:

1. **Level one** leaders are highly capable individuals who make productive contributions through knowledge, skills and good work habits.

2. **Level two** is where the team member contributes individual capabilities to the achievement of group objectives and works effectively with others in-group settings.

3. At **Level three** we have a competent manager who organises people and resources towards the effective and efficient pursuit of predetermined objectives.

4. At **Level four** we see an effective leader with a vigorous pursuit and a commitment to a clear and compelling vision, stimulating higher performance standards.

5. The **Level five** executive builds enduring greatness through a paradoxical blend of **personal humility and professional will.**

Note that Level 5 leadership goes against the grain of the common belief that an organisation or a Credit Union needs a larger than life professional with a big personality to transform a business. They are modest and willful, humble and fearless.

Modesty and humility are traits not often immediately evident in successful people, but when you look closer at a Level 5 CEO, it will be apparent. These are the leaders who tend to give credit to others while assigning blame to themselves.

Jim Collins and his team have compiled masses of research over his career. They selected 1,435 companies between 1965 and 1994 in the Fortune 500 listing. After screening these for patterns of above average returns, this was reduced down to 126 companies. There were eleven criteria on which these 126 companies were assessed which brought the numbers down to 19. Through a rigorous examination of these nineteen companies they eliminated Heinz, Kellogg's, Hershey, CPC, General Mills, Sara Lee, Coca-Cola and PepsiCo, such was the quality of the final eleven. Then they set about analysing the qualities of the leaders in those eleven organisations.

> 'You can accomplish anything in life, provided that you do not mind who gets the credit.'
> *(Harry S Truman)*

Collins makes the point that Level 5 leadership is not just about humility and modesty. It is equally about ferocious resolve, an almost **stoic determination** to do whatever must be done to get the job done and **make the company great**. They are fanatically driven to produce results and will **make tough decisions** for the good of the company.

So, can we learn how to be Level 5 leaders or are they born that way? It is likely that with the right supports and mentoring, some individuals have the potential to be leaders at this level. I should mention that not every Credit Union needs a leader of this calibre, as there are many CEO's who will achieve significant results with different skill sets.

It is fair to assume that when boards are hiring a new CEO, most will lean towards **confidence rather than competence**, and charisma rather than humility. For this reason, we do not often see Level 5 leaders at the top of an organisation. But that shouldn't prevent you from including at least one potential Level 5 leader in your management team, if you can find one. What would you give to have individuals on your management team or your board who, when things do not go as well as planned, look in the mirror and blame themselves? And when the right results flood in, they look outwards to give credit to the team and to outstanding colleagues who contributed to the success.

So, when we are looking at strategic leadership, we look inwards at our personal capacity to lead, we recognise our limitations, and we surround ourselves with the talents and skills needed to equip all stakeholders in the execution of the strategic plan. That is also to say that strategic leadership requires us to remove those in our vicinity who are unable or unwilling to excel as part of the management team. And equally, each manager is required to bring their team players up to a standard or disengage from them, if that is the best alternative option for the Credit Union.

Leaders with aspirations of reaching Level 5 status who already display considerable commitment and determination, should:

- recognise the difference between managing and leading
- work on their self-awareness
- improve their ability to control impulses, and to think before acting
- hone their networking and relationship skills
- empathise more
- maintain their passion and energy at optimum levels.

The world does not have too many Level 5s, and it's unlikely that your Credit Union will encounter an over-abundance of this rare species.

Succession Planning

There is one other aspect of strategic leadership that I want to cover here and that is the subject of **leadership pipeline** and **succession planning**. Many Credit Unions have people who work at the wrong level of leadership. For example, there may be a CEO who is frequently involved in the day-to-day direction of employees when there are managers or supervisors allocated to this role. Similarly there may be managers who spend much of their time doing the work that others are responsible for. Sometimes this is because the manager is more comfortable doing that type of work instead of managing. Unfortunately, this does not contribute to personal development for the manager or indeed for the employee who is prevented from doing his/her work.

In order to have a leadership pipeline, those budding leaders must move from the work they were doing and embrace a new form of behaviour. This requires a shift in skills and work values. New skills need to be developed and nurtured. This is best done through an external professional source where management skills can be assessed and enhanced. Unless the individual believes that this new type of work is more important than the work that was previously undertaken, there will continue to be an attachment and attraction to the earlier work patterns.

So, in order to develop an element of leadership pipeline, the CEO will be required to identify the potential in each of the middle management, and encourage these employees to develop personal attributes appropriate for the next role. In some instances this will involve coaching and mentoring an individual to take over the reins when the CEO has departed. In other instances it will require the next level of responsibility to identify suitable employees who have the potential to fill a management or supervisory role and begin the journey of developing that employee for promotion.

Succession planning should support strategic planning and strategic thinking. It should be regarded as an important tool for implementing strategic plans. It should provide an essential starting point for management and employee development programs. Without it, Credit Unions will have difficulty maintaining leadership continuity or identifying appropriate leaders when a change in business strategy is necessary. In its simplest form **succession planning is a form of risk management**. Rothwell from the American Management Association assures us that it goes beyond replacement planning. It is **proactive** and attempts to ensure continuity of leadership by cultivating talent from within an organisation through **planned development activities.**

Furthermore, succession planning refers more broadly to the ongoing process of identifying future leaders in an organisation and developing them so they are ready to move into leadership roles when required. Having this enabled should ensure that the Credit Union will have the right people in the right positions at the right time.

There is a growing importance of knowledge capital, and knowledge transfer. These are the **intangible assets** that represent valuable ideas, methods, processes and other intuitive talents that belong to a Credit Union. Indeed it is fair to say that much of a Credit Union's competitive advantage is in the unique combination of talent and knowledge within the HR capital. To permit this capital to dissipate or evaporate over time would be a travesty. Successful businesses recognise this and have programmes in place to transfer specialist knowledge to other team members in order to retain it in the organisation. Where a Credit Union has no such formal arrangement in place it should consider the likely disruption to the business in the event of an unexpected loss of key knowledge and key talent, and examine ways to formalise efforts in order to retain such knowledge within the Credit Union.

Consider taking the following steps:

- Assess the Credit Union and its future growth plans
- Determine the key leadership positions
- Identify core competencies for key positions
- Look at the pool of possible candidates and assess their likely fit for the roles
- Generate plans to develop individuals
- Monitor progress against agreed competencies

Most Credit Unions will be able to identify the key positions that must be filled in the event of a resignation, retirement or long-term illness. However it is important to keep an open mind beyond the CEO, CFO or COO. There are often valuable talents among the workforce that would be a serious loss to the Credit Union if an individual were to leave for any reason.

My final words in this section offer a question to you the reader. You can ask it of yourself, your managers, or your employees: **'What is it that you are currently working on to improve your personal performance or behaviour?'** When this question is answered honestly, it will lead to a better you. Strategy is not just for the business; it's as much for the individual as well.

The nature of life is that we are in a state of flux. Change will either be forced upon us or we will lead and direct the change ourselves. I will cover the topic of change management in more detail in the next chapter.

Reader's notes... ✍

There cannot be a crisis next week.
My schedule is already full.

Henry Kissinger

Love it or Loathe it, we are Going to CHANGE

As I mentioned in the previous chapter, **Insight** is the skill of understanding what is going on right now; **Foresight** is the skill of recognising future trends. A CEO or manager with a modicum of foresight will need to recognise the need for, and be at the forefront of leading change in an organisation. In the past ten years Credit Unions have probably changed more than in the previous forty years, and this rate of change may well continue, or accelerate.

When we experience change, we invariably need to examine the available resources, and decide if we can reallocate resources from the current supply, or if we need to acquire extra resources. The level of flexibility a Credit Union has in freeing up trapped resources when required is called **Resource Fluidity**.

As strategy involves execution, and change requires fluidity, then you need to plan ahead and bring all employees to a new standard or capability each year. An employee who is unable to undertake 90% of the duties of a Credit Union official is an untapped resource. Your Credit Union can not afford to have many individuals incapable or unwilling to carry out the duties of receptionist, teller, lending officer, credit controller, telephonist, administrator, insurance related services, foreign exchange and so on. The greater the level of capability among

90

the employees, the greater the resource fluidity will be.

'People don't resist change. They resist being changed.' Peter Senge, MIT based author, researcher and educator is credited with these words of wisdom.

This is one of the accepted principles in change management. It is also true that employees who frequently experience job enrichment and job rotation are familiar with the concept of change and can cope with change better than others who are in the same role for years.

> **People don't resist change. They resist BEING changed.**

There are many great books written on the subject of change. One charming book is: *'Who moved my Cheese'* by Spencer Johnson. It's a No. 1 best seller from the author of *'The One Minute Manager'*. I recommend this to every employee who hasn't read it yet, as it is short and sweet. The abiding message in the book is that things constantly change so **we must adapt**.

Another book is *'Our Iceberg is Melting'* by John Kotter and Holger Rathgeber. This is equally short and sweet and if you prefer you can show the ten-minute video to your team, as it's available on YouTube. The message is similar, insofar as nothing stays the same forever, and when you recognise the need for change, you must follow up with actions.

Kotter is the author of several publications on the subjects of change, strategy and leadership. He writes with Dan Cohen in their book *'The Heart of Change'* that there are eight steps to successful change and transforming your Credit Union:

1. **Increase Urgency**. Establishing and raising the feeling of urgency so that people tell each other 'we must do something' about the problems and opportunities. This reduces the fear and complacency that prevents change from starting.

2. **Build the Guiding Team.** Gathering the right group of people with the right attitudes and characteristics and authority to drive the change efforts.

3. **Get the vision right**. Helping the guiding team develop bold strategies for making courageous visions a reality. Facilitating the transition from analysis and financial plans to creating the right compelling vision and effort.

4. **Communicate for buy-in.** Sending clear, credible messages about the direction of change. Using words and actions to overcome confusion and mistrust. Using every means possible to communicate the new vision and strategies.

5. **Empower Action**. Removing barriers that block those who have genuinely embraced the new vision and strategies. Removing obstacles so that people can behave in a different way.

6. **Planning for and creating short-term wins.** Generate

enough wins as soon as possible to diffuse scepticism and pessimism. Make sure those successes are visible, unambiguous, and that they communicate what employees deeply care about. Recognise and reward employees who get involved in the improvements.

7. **Don't let up**. Help people to create wave after wave of change until the vision is a reality. Do not permit urgency to falter. Do not avoid the more difficult parts of the transformation, especially the bigger emotional barriers. Avoid physical and mental exhaustion by eliminating needless work

8. **Make the change stick.** Ensure that employees continue to act in the new ways, despite the pull of tradition. Reshape the organisational culture by re-rooting new behaviours. Enhance new norm values and shared emotions.

The first four steps aim to **unlock** or **un-freeze** the Credit Unions existing culture, firstly by creating a strong sense of **urgency for change**, secondly by assembling a powerful **group** to lead the change process, thirdly by developing a desirable **vision** of the future and fourthly by **communicating the vision** effectively.

Steps five, six and seven help to make the change a reality by **removing obstacles** to the vision, **creating short-term wins** and **consolidating successes**. The eighth and final step then **re-freezes** the Credit Union's new culture by **anchoring positive behaviours** into the new philosophy and values of the organisation.

Credit should be given to Kurt Lewin who originally put forward the three-step concept of Unfreezing, Changing, and Refreezing in 1951. There have been theories on change management for hundreds of years and it still boils down to the idea that people don't resist change; they resist being changed.

Kotter's approach is somewhat rigid in its style, as each step should be taken in turn. Sometimes a desire to stick too closely to the plan can in itself cause problems. It is therefore important to be aware of the bigger picture in your Credit Union throughout the change process, and to build some flexibility into your plans.

The second aspect to note on this approach is that the model describes a 'top-down' approach to change management. Depending on your Credit Union's size and the prevailing culture, a combination of top-down and bottom-up activities may be more appropriate. It can be very useful to bring small groups of employees into the picture at an early stage and ask for their suggestions as to how the vision for change could become reality in their work area.

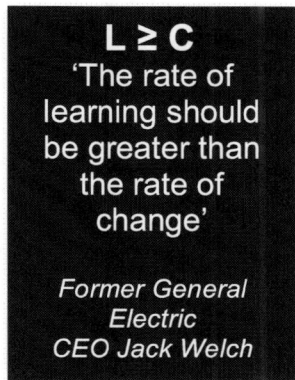

> ## $L \geq C$
> 'The rate of learning should be greater than the rate of change'
>
> *Former General Electric CEO Jack Welch*

The Soft Side

There is a psychology to the internal process of change that employees must undergo. Leaders who fail to recognise this soft side of the change process will invariably see for themselves why **most changes do not run smoothly**, or indeed fail outright.

The first stage of this psychological change is the requirement for employees to let go of the past and say cheerio to the status quo. You are sometimes asking employees to abandon the way they have successfully accomplished tasks in the past; to let go of trusted systems and work practices that they have honed and valued for years. People need time to consider their motivations and we can all appreciate that is it not easy to move on from familiar ground.

In the next stage we need to ask employees to move into the new world, they need to shift gears into neutral. This is a **time of confusion** for many, and the response will be to either revert to the past or to head boldly and quickly into the future. To help people through this stage of the transition we need to restate the vision, the reasons for the change, and outline the part that each employee will play in the new role.

The third stage, where we move forward into the new world is also a psychological challenge for many people. We need to recognise that it will be a **time of uncertainty** and perhaps there will be a lack of confidence. Employees will recall that poor performance has historically been penalised, so some will hold back to see how others progress.

It can be said that **not every change is an improvement but every improvement is a change**. Hence any improvement will be met with varying degrees of resistance, which no doubt you will have recognised in different people at different times.

To conclude this section, the following are some signs of resistance to change:

- Displaying a **defensive attitude** or becoming withdrawn when changes are mentioned.

- Identifying **complications** with proposed changes but not offering any solutions.

- **Negative body language** when discussing change.

- Constantly **complaining** to colleagues about the planned changes.

- **Picking** on minor elements of the change.

- Purposely **dropping standards** of productivity when working on duties associated with the change.

It is essential to recognise these signs in individuals, and rather than chastise them for being negative, reassure them with practical support. In fact you should encourage the sceptics, because they will quickly identify the problem issues for you, and you will not be left guessing for long.

> 'It's not the strongest of the species who survive, nor the most intelligent, but the ones most responsive to change'
> *Charles Darwin*

If you are honest in your dealings with people, clear in your communications, and provide regular opportunities for employees to question the change, then you will have a better than average chance of succeeding with the change project.

Oh, and 'one more thing' as Detective Columbo used to say. If the world outside is changing at a faster pace than your world inside, then you are not even standing still. You are losing ground. Change must be embedded in your culture, and that requires a significant range of skills from the CEO as well as the entire workforce in your Credit Union.

Reader's notes...

Change will not come if we wait for some other person or some other time.
We are the ones we've been waiting for.
We are the change that we seek.

Barack Obama

Business Model Canvas

When a colleague or stakeholder asks you 'So what is your business model?' you are really being questioned on how your Credit Union plans to generate enough income to meet your overheads and provide a surplus for future development and reserves. Business models are an essential part of strategy as they provide for the future sustainability of the business.

A Credit Union business model can be described with nine basic building blocks:

1. **Your member segments.** These are all the members in different segments for whom you are creating value. They may be young or old, students or working, male or female, homeowners or renters, active and inactive and so on. Which segments or classes are you creating value for? Who are your most important members?

2. **Your value proposition**. For each different segment, you will have a different or similar value proposition. What is the core value that you deliver to your members? Which member needs are you satisfying? How do you capture value from those transactions?

3. **The channels to reach members**. This describes through which touch points you interact with different members. Some channels are face to face, others are through social media, and more are via intermediaries or business

introducers. Which channels work best? What distribution channels do your members prefer? How much do these channels cost?

4. **The member relationships** you establish outline the type of rapport you have with the different member segments. What level of relationship do different member groupings expect?

5. **The revenue streams** you generate. This shows your pricing structure and how you capture value and generate income. For what value are your members willing to pay? How would they prefer to pay? How much does each revenue stream contribute to the overall revenues of the Credit Union?

6. **The key resources** you require to create and capture value. What traditional and technological infrastructure do you need to operate this business model? Which resources are the most important? Which ones can you contract out more efficiently than can be hired in?

7. **Key activities** outline which activities you need to perform well in order to deliver the desired member experience. Which activities are the most important? Which activities generate revenue and which ones generate costs?

8. Identifying your **Key partners** will shows you who can help you leverage your business model. What are the motivations for the partnerships? Which partners could you cultivate further to enhance your business?

9. **The cost structure** of the business model. How do you review costs and budgets? Which overheads are likely to increase in the next twelve months? What costs are fixed or variable?

These building blocks can be mapped out on a pre-structured canvas, and this is called the **business model canvas**. It is helpful to outline your entire business model on one page, and this works just as well for a small Credit Union as it does for a significant Credit Union. A pre-designed format is available on the web from Strategyzer.com. Credit to the original developer and designer of the business model canvas, **Alexander Osterwalder**, who also co-founded Strategyzer.com.

The following page shows Osterwalder's blank canvas with the nine headings pre-populated.

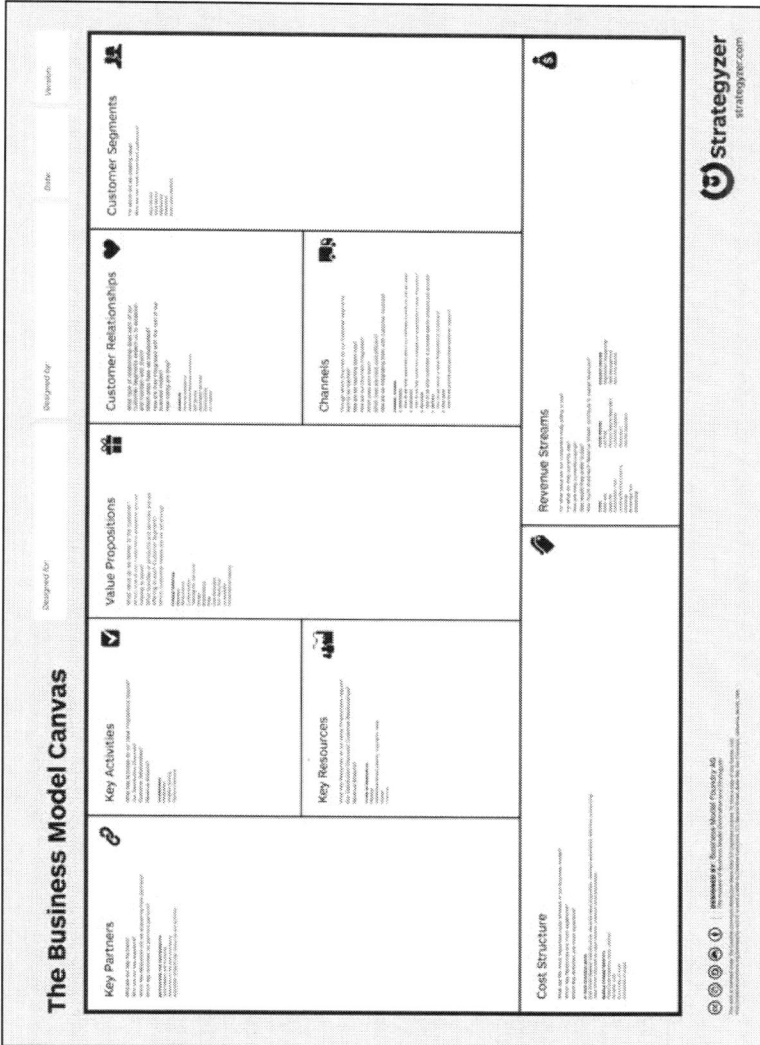

Whatever way you view your business model, you need to challenge it for **durability and sustainability**. What was good enough two years ago, or even last month, may not be

102

fully suitable for the next twelve months and beyond. The life cycle of products and services is getting shorter, so a product will be obsolete sooner now than it might have been in the past. The perfect example is the mobile phone, which continues to be reinvented every six months. Online banking and money transmission are two other examples of services that continue to evolve.

When you review the different elements of your business model, it is tempting to feel satisfied that each component is working just fine. It may be fine right now and for the short term, but the trouble with taking the short-term solution is that you STOP looking for long-term results. In other words you take your eyes off the prize. In fact, **if everything is** deemed to be **satisfactory** for you and your Credit Union right now, you are in a **dangerous place**, because you will not see change coming when your guard is down.

For those readers who may be unconvinced about the value of a one-page business model canvas, let me mention three distinct advantages of using this approach.

1. *Emphasis.* Traditional business plans tend to have reams of filler pages. Possibly forty or fifty pages that you could really do without. The sort of content that you tend to skim over. The business model canvas forces you to be **precise** in identifying exactly what is generating the business, what resources are in place or needed, and the defining value proposition. Ask yourself what is so unique about the member experience in your Credit Union?

2. *Pliability*. Think about how easy is it to make adjustments to the content of one page, compared to re-defining your plans across a fifty-plus page document with appendices and cross references? Simply adjusting the wording on a few key phrases can dramatically alter the power of the page.

3. *Clarity*. You and your team will have no difficulty understanding the contents of one page. But be assured that distilling an entire business plan or business model onto one page is no mean feat. It is much easier to take the traditional route and continue typing until every thought is down on paper.

Whether you chose to share a one-page plan with your team and wider stakeholders, or prefer other communication tools, you must ensure that the business model is appropriate for the future sustainability of the Credit Union. The pace of change is accelerating and the external market conditions regularly present fresh challenges. Today's business models in any sector are vulnerable and require frequent review and evaluation.

Credit Unions are known more for their consistency and reliability, than for their groundbreaking innovations. The future requires more than consistency, and many Credit Unions are operating a dated business model that warrants significant change to meet the business demands of tomorrow.

Reader's notes... ✍

> I don't measure a mans success by how high
> he climbs, but how high he bounces
> when he hits bottom.
>
> *George S Patton*

Value Proposition

Value proposition is a phrase that is used more and more in Credit Unions. It is sometimes mistaken for your unique selling proposition (USP) but that is only part of your value proposition. In its simplest terms, a value proposition is the overall perceived value of your Credit Union service and products, including everything that your members believe is valuable in your offering to them. So, it identifies what **benefits you provide** for members and how you do it **uniquely well**. It describes your target audience, your specific member groups, the problems you solve, and **why you're distinctly better** than the others who supply a similar service.

Identifying and determining your Credit Union's core value proposition is not an easy task. Most CEOs will make the point that their Credit Union is good at **all** aspects of the value proposition. The idea is that you need to be **exceptionally good** at **one of them** in order for this to distinguish you from all the other competition.

There are three classic value propositions:

1. **Product Leadership.** This is where organisations have the leading products in the market. They compete on **innovation and speed** of delivery. Customers or members expect the latest state of the art innovation and are often brand loyal to those companies. The best way to win here is to be first to market as often as possible. If a

Credit Union were in this space, then nothing would get close to the quality of loan, savings and insurance products it provides. It is fair to say that most Credit Unions would not categorise product leadership as their value proposition.

2. **Operational Excellence**. This is where you have stripped out virtually all the costs and operate a **lean business**. Your overheads are significantly less than those of your competitors. It is unusual and unlikely to see this type of operation in a traditional business, i.e. a business or organisation that has been around for many years, or a business with a relatively high staff costs/income ratio. These lean businesses shy away from HR costs, and often have little or no fixed asset overheads. The low costs allow the organisation to offer its services at a low price to the consumer, and still maintain strong operating margins.

3. **Customer Intimacy.** These businesses compete on the basis of quality customer service and **customer relationship**. Credit Unions are excellent in this area and develop a relationship with members as a matter of priority. The objective here is to gain the member for life and be the premier provider of financial services to them throughout their lifetime. These customers or members are interested in getting exactly what they want, even if that means they have to pay a little more than elsewhere. When members find they can get solutions to their problems, from people who know them well, with professional and personal service, they will give the Credit

Union their loyalty in return.

For most, if not all Credit Unions, the value proposition will be in the area of member intimacy. It doesn't really matter where you are, how large or small your business is, or what your value proposition is. **What does matter is that you have one and you execute it.** That said you still have room to expand your operational excellence by playing your cards differently, or more efficiently.

> The value you offer to members is not the price or the product. It is the *trust and personal service*.

A well thought out value proposition may stand the test of time for many years, however this is dependent on the speed of change externally and internally. A Level 5 CEO will know when to adjust or strengthen the value proposition. Consider the consequence for your community if you were to close your Credit Union. **To what extent would your community miss you? What is it that they value in your Credit Union today, that they would be deprived of if you were gone tomorrow?**

Once defined and articulated, the value proposition needs to be communicated to every employee, volunteer, and board member in the Credit Union. In so doing you will ensure as far as possible that each individual knows what part they have to play in delivering on the strategic goals. Your managers will also take steps to review the processes, policies, and reward systems to ensure that these are aligned to the value proposition and the overall strategy.

All stakeholders in your Credit Union must effectively sign up to being the best in class, better than all the competitors, and recognised as the number one provider of financial services in your defined market place or common bond.

Once you get to this stage it is necessary to have the commitment from all concerned that you will look to improve every aspect of your business on a regular basis regardless of whether you believe it's working well or not. There can be no room for complacency, even when you are voted the best by the media, by members, and admired by competitors. Every service provider looks to be number one, and you can be certain that others are taking steps to replace you on that podium position. Your job is to get to the number one spot and stay there. Understanding your value proposition will help you in that endeavour.

In their book *Discipline of Market Leaders'*, Michael Treacy and Fred Wiersema expand on the new world of competition. They argue that there are four new premises underlying successful business practice today:

- Companies can **no longer raise prices** in tandem with higher costs; they have to try to lower costs to accommodate rising customer expectations.

- Companies can no longer aim for anything less than **hassle-free service.** Their customers enjoy effortless, flawless, and instantaneous performance from one industry and expect it from every other sector across all industries.

109

- Companies can no longer assume that good basic service is enough; members demand **premium service** – and raise their expectations continuously.

- Companies can no longer compromise on quality and product capabilities. They must build products and services to deliver nothing less than superiority and **eye-popping innovation.**

These are four compelling statements to ponder. The concept of offering hassle free service is well put and members expect this in so many ways. We expect it ourselves when dealing with suppliers in our personal lives. Unfortunately, when we take a long hard look at the services we currently offer members, there are elements that might not be described as hassle free, and we need to do something about this.

As a Credit Union we need to ask ourselves if we can **innovate the value rather than the product.** In how many ways can we add value to the service and the member experience? After all, we are taking deposits and lending those monies out at a fair margin to cover costs and future investment in the business. It's a straightforward business. The challenge is to innovate the value proposition, and there are many ways to approach this so that you widen the difference between your Credit Union and other service providers.

For example you could add value in your Credit Union by offering a free one-hour consultation with the business manager or the marketing officer, or one of your qualified financial advisors. Maybe you could offer a half-day on-site

110

visit to a business or a community enterprise once a fortnight? There are many initiatives that your employees could suggest, or better still, you could ask your members for their suggestions. You get very few opportunities to tell members what you stand for, so give them the compliment of asking them for their input. Simply asking this of your members is a sign of respect and in itself will differentiate you from other financial services providers.

Many well established clubs and organisations in your area would appreciate the opportunity to meet a loans officer and your marketing officer some evening. You could offer help and ideas for fundraising, talk about borrowing, and give them some pointers on how they might better manage their financials.

The more value you can offer to your members, the stronger your value proposition is, and the longer you will hold that number one spot. It is important to move your thinking away from 'product' and more towards 'value'. There is an increasing list of product suppliers in the financial services industry, but there should be only one provider of the value you offer your members.

This begs several questions:
- 'Why do so many of your members discontinue their relationship with you?'
- Is there a reason why members open an account with you and then use their bank for services that you can offer?
- Have you done enough to stay in touch with members?

111

- If your value proposition is so great, why are you not the first choice loan provider for every member?

These are questions we all have to address, and once you step into your members' shoes and see their needs you will begin to understand the reasons why you are not always the first choice provider of personal finance.

Coca Cola decided to remove all the clutter regarding the planning process and emerging businesses, so employees were charged with a single job function: 'Sell More Coke'. What would your Credit Union's 'single function' be? Make members happy? Improve member's wellbeing? Grow the loan book? Increase net surplus? It's always difficult to distill down to a single page, especially a single sentence, but if you are looking for your core purpose or core objective, it is an imperative.

Another option is to look at the companies or businesses that have made you a satisfied customer? And what are the ones that made you a dis-satisfied customer? I recall being part of a service-excellence training day when the facilitator posed this question. It was interesting to see that not one of the fifty attendees mentioned price as the reason for being satisfied or dissatisfied. It will be the same for the majority of your members insofar as their pain and gain stories about your Credit Union. I refer to 'pain' as a metaphor for the reason why members use their Credit Union, and the 'gain' as the solution offered to the members to solve the problem, i.e. remove the pain.

Consequently, an essential ingredient in value proposition is **Expectation**. You must manage the business so as to at least meet your members' expectations, and understand that expectations are driven up by good service. As a result, the better you are, the better you need to become. If you are not exceeding expectations you are not differentiating your business and other companies will eventually be seen as the same as you. It's good to keep moving the bar upwards so as to make it increasingly more difficult for competition to match you. Your members must expect more from you than they expect from anyone else, and then that expectation must be delivered on. That is the challenge you and your employees must be up for, day in day out.

Once you and your team have a strong appreciation of your Credit Unions value proposition, it is worthwhile viewing the business from the members' perspective as well as from within the Credit Union. The following chapter addresses these viewpoints.

Reader's notes... ✍

> When your work speaks for itself,
> don't interrupt.
>
> *Henry J Kaiser*

Looking Out and Looking In

Adrian J Slywotzky has written an impressive book on how to think several moves ahead of the competition, and he calls it 'value migration'. According to Slywotzky, **'value migration'** is the flow of economic and shareholder value away from an increasingly outmoded business design toward others that are better equipped to create value for customers/members and profit for the company. That's quite a mouthful, but essentially it refers to the concept of losing business to another supplier who is now doing a better job than you in meeting the needs of the consumer.

Sometimes this occurs over several years and is not evident to those inside the company. It's a little like the way an individual will age over time: it's only really apparent when you compare the photo from ten years ago to todays image. But during that period, there is no single identifiable instance that points to that person getting older.

So, we look outwards to keep tabs on the disruption in the market place and how the 'disrupters' change habits. Recent arrivals such as Airbnb and Uber have changed the way many consumers book accommodation and taxis. And there is a common theme among these new 'disrupters'. In the main, they do not acquire fixed assets, as their business models are supported by easily accessed technologies, aka mobile phones. And they rely on 'free' social media rather than 'paid for' advertising.

115

The traditional business model of Credit Unions is also under threat from 'disrupters' who are in the lending business without branches or deposits, and have minimal human resources. Their strategy is to link people and businesses that wish to borrow, with individuals who want to lend. They provide the technological infrastructure to enable the transactions to take place, and earn a modest margin on the transactions. We all lend our spare money to Credit Unions and banks, and we call this saving. The same savers are now lending their money to businesses and generating an improved return, with a slight increase in risk.

It is useful to regularly look outside the Credit Union and ensure that you are not in denial of industry trends.

- Who in your Credit Union takes an interest in the external environment and keep tabs on new and emerging trends?

- How do you and your board react to this wave of trends?

Navel-Gazing (noun)

'Self-indulgent or excessive contemplation of oneself or a single issue, at the expense of a wider view'.

- Do you accept that it is highly unlikely that your members will be transacting with you in the same way in five years or less?

- What actions are planned to adjust and fine-tune your strategy and business model in order to cope with these events?

You should ask this of yourself because there is an inherent risk of failure if you just look inwards.

Gathering information on external changes in the market place and making sure that all employees are up to speed will help to ensure that employees are not insulated from the real world, which is very often the case.

When you look inwards you may discover that you have the wrong value offering. Perhaps you are effective but not agile. By agile I mean that you are capable and resourced well enough to respond quickly to changing trends. In modern parlance are you **Mission Ready**? McKinsey & Co describes it as, 'the capacity to identify and capture opportunities more quickly than rivals do'.

They also talk about turbulence in the market and this generally refers to the emergence of disruptors as mentioned above. McKinsey & Co says, 'Turbulence is a measure of the frequency of unpredictable changes affecting the ability of companies to create and sustain value'.

Another reason for looking in from the outside is to step into the needs of non-members. It is really important to see and hear the views of people in the community who do not buy from you or see you as relevant. The same can be said of existing members who for many reasons do not fully use Credit Union services. You need to better understand what is missing from the relationship and how you can address it. Is it a weakness or shortcoming in your offering, or is there a stronger pull towards other financial services suppliers?

A successful Credit Union will find it difficult to accept that there may be stormy waters ahead, or that the business may decline because the strategy was lacking an external focus. Those Credit Unions generating an annual increase of 10% or 20% in revenue should know that **past growth is no indicator of any future growth.** It is much better to have a discussion around the fundamental strategy that underpins the future business growth assumptions. The lazy approach is to assume that this year will be the same as last year if you do the same as before. That is a recipe for disaster. Unfortunately, this recipe has worked so well for so long that some boards and managers may believe it is a strategy in itself.

Looking out from the inside and looking in from the outside is more about anticipating future trends and less about satisfying stakeholders.

No matter how well your Credit Union is doing, you cannot afford to overlook the emerging trends externally, and occasionally you should take a look at your Credit Union from a non-users perspective. Or better still, engage someone to independently look at your Credit Union and your competitors through the lens of a non-member.

There are too many examples of world-class products and services that were market leaders and are now extinct. You may recall some or all of these:

- **Atari games** were the world leaders in console games in the late 1970's and early 1980's. It virtually crashed in 1984.

- In the financial world the largest bankruptcy in the United States saw the demise of **Lehman Brothers** who were established in 1840. It was the biggest company to fail during the last financial crash.

- **Blockbuster movie** rental is often quoted as a business that was extremely successful but did not look outwards very often. Although not completely disappeared it failed to recognise the emerging trends for streaming content, like Netflix, MUBI and similar services.

- **Kodak** practically invented the digital camera but waited too long because they thought it would kill their existing business. In 2012 they filed for bankruptcy.

- By the time **Woolworth's** was 100 years old it was the world's largest department store chain. It was declared bankrupt in 1997 following the success of Wall Mart and other competitors. I remember there being a Woolworth's store in every city and town in the UK. Slowly but surely their business model was copied by others, which is what businesses do when they target whoever is in the number one spot.

- **Pan American** World Airways were the industry leader with the tagline 'World's most experienced airline'. It folded in 1991 following increasing competition and pressure on fuel prices. This is an industry that has undergone an incredible transformation. When I first moved to London in 1974 it cost a month's wages to fly from London to Dublin, so I could not afford to travel home as often as I would have liked. Now, the same journey can be purchased for a fraction of that cost, and todays airlines are highly profitable with a business model that offer low prices.

- In 1972, **Polaroid** launched the SX-70; the first fully integrated instant camera and film system, hailed by Fortune magazine as one of the greatest industrial inventions of the time. The company was founded in 1937 and yet it filed for bankruptcy protection in October 2001 and again in December 2008. Its stock price had declined from $50 to 28 cents. The advancement of digital photography marked the point at which Polaroid's decline was never to recover from. It still exists in another form and has developed Polaroid Snap for instant digital photos.

These are classic cases of business believing that it has conquered the world and will never be overtaken. They could have looked out to see what was approaching on the horizon. A mistake for any company for sure. In fact this state of mind is often described as the most dangerous for any business that is considered to be at the top of its game.

We must accept that no business or organisation is completely immune from failure, but it does help if someone is watching for signs of change internally and externally and anticipating how strategy might be adjusted in response to or in advance of market changes.

I am reminded of the famous question that the hotel waiter asked George Best as he delivered champagne to the room and George was entertaining Miss World, with thousands of pounds of casino winnings strewn across the bedroom. 'Where did it all go wrong?' he asked.

It was years later that Best observed 'Perhaps he saw something in me that I hadn't seen in myself'. This is the very essence of many examples where businesses were apparently very successful, yet fell into oblivion some years later.

So it is important not to be insulated or isolated from the external environment. Keeping a constant focus on the horizon will ensure a balanced view, as well as standing back occasionally and looking into your Credit Union from the standpoint of a non-member. You could do worse than ask a trusted colleague from your professional network if they would be the eyes and ears of your non-member and provide you with valuable feedback from time to time. Indeed you could possibly reciprocate the favour, and learn something about another business in the process.

Reader's notes... ✍

> There is nothing like looking,
> if you want to find something.
>
> *JRR Tolkien, The Hobbit*

Moore's Law

In 1965, a physicist named Gordon Moore observed that silicon chips were getting more powerful and smaller. He predicted that by 1975 the computing power would have doubled every year, so that 'an integrated circuit could be built on a single wafer' (a wafer being a small chip), containing 65,000 components and eventually be cheap enough to produce and sell that computers would be widely available.

His friend, a professor at the California Institute of Technology dubbed this **'Moore's Law'**. Apart from an adjustment to the time period, i.e. from doubling every year to every two years, this has proven true.

In the 1990s professional standards in the semi conductor industry even started to revolve around Moore's Law, as a roadmap for technological development.

Samsung, Intel and Microsoft, three of the largest IT companies, spent $37 billion between them on R&D in 2015.

By the year 2000, chips had components that were 180 nanometers wide (a nanometer is a billionth of a meter). By 2016, they were down to 14 nano's wide! Recently I met an engineer who works in the medical devices industry and they supply equipment worldwide that dispenses medicines in Pico dimensions, which are even smaller than Nano.

Computing power will continue to evolve at a rapid pace, and we know that what seems 'normal' now, seemed impossible 30 years ago. Furthermore, what seemed normal 30 years ago seems pre-historic now.

The pace of change in the external environment must be equalled in our internal environment, i.e. within our own Credit Unions. It is part of our differentiation that we can hold on to long standing values, however that should not preclude us from grasping new opportunities, and staying relevant to our entire membership. Some members value the traditional service channels and other members place a high reliance on technological advancement, or at least staying abreast with what is considered standard offerings in today's markets. That is the challenge, in the face of Moore's Law!

I mention Moore's Law because we sometimes do not recognise the pace of change in our own Credit Union movement and in the financial services sector. It's easy to recognise the speed of change in personal computers and other similar technologies. But ask an eighty-year-old member if they can keep up to date with the pace of change and you will get some interesting answers. Most elderly members will tell you that there have been more significant advancements in their lifetime than there were in the previous ten centuries. It is a fact of life and it is unlikely to slow down.

There are significant changes afoot in 3D printing, the Internet of Things, and virtual reality. These technologies will displace many industries and businesses in the same way that the smart phone displaced or enhanced diaries, cameras, small

124

torches, mini calculators, the GPS and how we listen to music or do our banking. We need to be prepared for the day that substitute suppliers will attempt to displace Credit Unions, or perhaps displace those Credit Unions who are ill prepared for change.

Moores Law is alive and well and we need to factor it into our strategic thinking.

Reader's notes...

One machine can do the work of fifty ordinary
men. No machine can do the work of one
extraordinary man.

Elbert Hubbard (Author)

Suppliers

As this entire book relates to the strategy of your Credit Union, think for a moment on how much you rely on the performance of the businesses you contract in to assist in executing your strategy.

The most obvious ones are your information technology suppliers, the website designers and Webmaster, your telecoms provider, various marketing suppliers, internal and external auditors, and legal and HR advisors.

There are many other less obvious suppliers such as your stationers, painters and decorators, electrical and other trades people. The security and alarm suppliers and monitoring station, as well as the fire alarm suppliers.

In fact every company or individual who provides a product or service, or in any way helps your Credit Union to function throughout the year, can be classed as a supplier.

Each of these in turn should be capable of contributing in a positive way towards your Credit Union's strategy. Perhaps you have discussed your business needs with your IT supplier and had a conversation or two with your marketing suppliers. But you may not have considered what part each supplier could play, including the man who changes the light bulbs or the cleaner who shines the floor for the members each morning. They all have a part to play.

127

So, you could share your aspirations with them and ask how they can contribute towards your goals and objectives. At the very least, they will have a better understanding as to why you are always looking to improve the member experience in the greater sense of the word. Your Credit Union might be the only business that asks that particular supplier to help in reaching milestones and achieving objectives, and you could have an advocate that will feel empowered to 'go the extra mile' or make a little difference to help with the bigger picture.

There are untapped resources at your disposal and you should seek to share the strategy with as many of your suppliers as possible. It is very likely that they are members already, and will speak more confidently of their Credit Union once they have a sense of being more involved and connected.

You will NOT execute your strategic plan without the support of your suppliers; so get them on the bus and share your destination map with them.

From time to time you will need to sever links with a supplier because they do not meet the standards you agreed. They may have simply let you down once too often or failed to deliver to an agreed specification. Better to take that action sooner rather than later, before further damage is done to your Credit Union brand.

From a strategy perspective you want your suppliers to be tuned into the aspirations and objectives of your Credit

Union, but you also want to know that they have the financial capability to deliver. Request their most recent annual accounts or consider using an appropriate agency to obtain a copy of them. Examine their financial statements in the same way your loans officer would scrutinise a members business accounts. Ask for feedback from other businesses that use these suppliers. Keep your ear to the ground. If any supplier subcontracts to another supplier in order to provide the product or service to you, it is sound practice to examine the accounts of these companies too.

When I worked in the catering industry, it was incumbent on our business to conduct regular inspections on the delivery vehicles, and to visit the premises of each supplier and record how well they maintained their business. In that industry the system is HACCP (Hazard Analysis Critical Control Point), and every restaurant, hotel and catering supplier is required by law to have a food safety management system in place.

The management system should allow operators to identify and control any hazards that could pose a danger to the preparation of safe food. It involves identifying what can go wrong, planning to prevent it and making sure that actions are taken where needed. In the same way, a Credit Union needs to identify what any and all likely risks are, and prepare for actions that will mitigate those risks. Understanding the strengths and weaknesses of your suppliers is one technique of identifying risks.

129

There are four types of risk mitigation:

- Accept the risk
- Avoid the risk altogether
- Take some action to limit the risk
- Transfer the risk

Using a supplier is in itself partly transferring the risk, but the most common practice from these four options is the third one: taking actions to limit the risk.

Considering the value you place in your Credit Union suppliers, and the trust you have in their ability to deliver what is needed, you should consider allocating an 'annual supplier check' role to a designated employee. This should be an open arrangement with your supplier, and if they resist any such system of checking, you probably have your answer already!

Ensure that your suppliers are fit for purpose, and replace those who are unfit to contribute to your strategic plan or elements of it.

Reader's notes... ✍

We've got to make the small things unforgettable.

Steve Jobs

CFO Function

Because Credit Unions come in varying sizes and shapes, it is likely that the Chief Financial Officer (CFO) will be responsible for different elements of the strategic plan depending on the size and shape of the Credit Union. For the most part, it's a role that evolves with the development and growth of a Credit Union's business over time.

A CFO will often attract functions because of inherent skills and aptitudes. From a strategy perspective, can you be assured that the role matches the needs of the business? Or have you simply allowed the role to develop into something that was never intended?

Typical functions of a CFO are the preparation and reporting of timely financial accounts, management accounting, payroll, treasury operations, banking, and supplier payments.

This narrow role is somewhat dated, as CFOs are now expected to contribute to the business in a more positive way by adding value to the strategic planning process and review of same, overseeing the collection of reluctant payers in credit control, providing the technical expertise relating to compliance and information technology, and generally ensuring that the Credit Union takes a balanced view on risk and reward.

Today's CFOs are expected to be leaders in performance

management, and need to have the range of skills that contribute to a balanced management team. Research has shown that a significant number of CFOs in global businesses have MBA's or other advanced degrees, and fewer tend to have accounting degrees (McKinsey – Today's CFOs). Many CFOs develop a reputation for transforming organisations and promote the use of metrics and scorecards. These individuals tend to have served their time internationally, or within different industries.

In short, your Credit Union should have a CFO that meets the needs of the organisation and complements the composition of the management team.

The CEO should question if the finance department and the CFO have targets to add value to the Credit Union, or are they there merely as goalkeepers and reporters. Each business unit in a Credit Union should be capable of adding value, and the CEO should be able to measure that value; if you cannot measure it then it does not exist. A friend who served on the board used

> 'Today's CFO's are engaged, focused, versatile, and strategic.'
>
> *EY (The evolving role of the CFO)*

to chant, 'what gets measured, gets done', and I'm sure he wasn't the first to coin that phrase. If the CFO is already adding value, then it may be possible to look at how further value could be added, and there are many ways this can be done.

133

The real value in a Credit Union or in any business is not so much in the balance sheet, but rather in future cash flows. Understanding the organisation's dynamics in optimising those cash flows requires a capable, experienced, analytical, and rounded strategist. A strong CFO will provide the balance required should this be in short supply or over supply with the incumbent Chief Executive. Indeed the specific profile of your CFO may need to be different from that of other Credit Unions, and determined by the strengths and challenges of the rest of the management team and the direction in which the business is headed.

Reader's notes... ✍

Money is better than poverty if only for financial reasons.

Woody Allen

Decision Making

Ok, we all know that strategy revolves around where we are now and where we are going. But what if the direction we are headed in is based on a polite consensus of the board and management team? Or perhaps a general agreement of the current position, which is in fact an ill-advised view of the position today?

Unconscious collusion occurs in management teams or boards where we agree not to upset each other. This curtails the learning process and stifles creativity. Throughout my varied career I have been lucky enough to be involved in teams where individuals express themselves without fear of ridicule or reprisal. This is where the gold nuggets are. For onlookers, this can appear to be a hostile environment, and at times it does become heated. On the other hand, there is little chance of finding gold nuggets in a room of nodding heads.

> Strategic decision-making is not always rational.

There are four different stages of team development: Forming, Storming, Norming, Performing. Would you believe that this dates back to 1965 when Dr. Bruce Tuckman, a psychology professor in Princeton University published his theory? It's called 'Storming' for a reason, and it can take time to develop a healthy decision making team.

Before you reroute the Credit Union in a fresh direction, it's vital that the team has experienced some uncomfortable exchange of views. At minimum there needs to be the 'eternal pessimist', the 'creative thinker', the 'give me the facts' guy, and the 'anything is possible' person. These individuals will help to ignite the 'storming' process, which is necessary to enable the team to grow and face up to the many challenges, tackle problems, look for various options and solutions, and finally agree a direction.

We tend to always think that the way we work together is the best way, so it is most unusual to witness a team actively looking for alternative ways to conduct business. The old saying, 'if it's not broken, don't fix it' is a strong argument in many boardrooms and at many management tables. It takes a brave team to reflect on how to improve the quality of meetings, participation levels, and decision-making.

When the CEO or Chairperson makes a significant decision, they rely somewhat on the judgment of the team who put forward the pros and cons for a strategic course of action. That team will often be so enamoured with its recommendations that biases creep in and distort logical thinking. They can subconsciously dismiss evidence that contradicts their views or give too much credence to one item of data. This is referred to as **team think**, or **confirmation bias**. Knowing that these preconceptions exist is not enough, because we invariably do not see our own biases.

A study of 1,000 business investments by McKinsey has shown that when companies worked to reduce the effects of bias, they raised their returns on investment by 7%. The decision making process should be disciplined, to ensure that decisions are based on all the available information, and the brilliance of one individual should not be the over-riding factor in determining which strategic direction to take.

Nobel-winning Princeton professor Daniel Kahneman, Sydney University professor Dan Lovallo, and McKinsey director Olivier Sibony recommend a decision making checklist to avoid the various traps, as follows:

1. Check for **self-interested biases.**

2. Check if the team **fell in love** with its own recommendation.

3. Check for **groupthink** and if dissenting voices were stifled.

4. Check if the recommendation was overly influenced by a **comparable situation.**

5. Check for **confirmation bias**. Were alternative options considered or was one option chosen and evidence collected to support that proposal?

6. Check for **availability bias**. Was it assumed that what we saw was all there is to see?

7. Check for **anchoring bias**. Is there an over reliance on one or two pieces of information.

8. Check for the **halo effect**. Just because an individual is brilliant in one area does not mean the person will be equally as brilliant in all areas.

9. Check if the recommendation is overly attached to **past decisions.**

10. Check for **over-confidence** by adopting an outsider's perspective.

11. Check for disaster neglect by conducting a **pre-mortem.**

12. Check for **loss aversion,** where a team may be overly cautious.

These insights underline the potential benefits of constructive dialogue in decision-making. Without the devil's advocate input or the frequent challenge to the various assumptions, there is the strong possibility that poor decisions will be made, albeit well intentioned.

This can be challenging for a Credit Union that experiences success because achievement usually solidifies our view of what works and we can be blinkered as to what is going on externally.

Reader's notes... ✍

If all the economists were laid end to end,
they'd never reach a conclusion.

George Bernard Shaw

Scenarios

The origins of scenarios are in warfare so there is no shortage of literature on the topic. Napoleon and Churchill were great strategists and used scenario planning to forecast likely outcomes of battles and future events.

At their lowest level, scenarios allow managers and management teams to develop a range of possible outcomes. Traditionally it was accepted that the past would dictate the future, or at least resemble it. In todays changing climate it is important to at least accept that there are circumstances which could quickly bring about a less favourable environment or set of circumstances.

Supply and demand are two scenarios that can be examined. Simple economics informs us that when demand falls off, the price usually reduces as well. We have seen this with interest rates; where money is in short supply the financial markets will pay a higher price to attract deposits. Conversely, when money is in over supply mode, it can even lead to negative interest rates.

Changes in local population as well as employment trends are somewhat predictable, and are useful scenarios to start with. Is there a local employer that is likely to expand its operations, or is there one that may be relocated or become obsolete? We are familiar with the devastating consequence for communities when a large established employer moves its operations out of

141

a location. The knock-on effect to a local Credit Union is a scenario worth contemplating, albeit uncomfortable to imagine.

In most cities there are companies employing thousands of members and Credit Unions should know at any time what the total exposure to each employer is, should that employer disengage from the locality. The strategy of continuing to increase the Credit Unions exposure should be weighed against the risks associated with a few scenarios. It may be that your absolute risk for loans to employees of a single employer is 10% of your loan book, or 5% of your assets or some such level. As ever, there is usually a greater risk to your business if you were to eliminate the risk entirely, rather than agree your appetite for risk in the face of possible scenarios.

Scenario analysis will help to encourage your Credit Union to be alert for different possibilities. The intention is not to accurately predict the future, but to **build strategies to cope with the impact of possible future scenarios.**

Depending on where you are in the economic cycle, it's likely that you will be pessimistic at the bottom of the cycle and conversely looking very positive while at the top of the trend. It is important to remind ourselves that upswings and downturns don't last forever, and an element of reality should be factored into any scenario. With the best will in the world, every business will occasionally meet obstacles and challenges, from within the organisation or caused by external factors.

When planning the release of a new service or product, you are invariably optimistic about where you slot the 'go live' date in the strategic plan. One scenario to consider is to push that date out beyond what is considered reasonable. No right thinking CEO will consider that deadlines are there to be missed, but this exercise will show the effects of losing the initiative, and reinforce the need to hit the agreed dates. It is not beyond the laws of possibility that forces will dictate a delay from time to time. These are 'unknown unknowns'. You can usually cope with the 'known knowns', and the 'known unknowns' but that's as far as most people's coping skills tend to stretch.

Scenarios help to protect against 'sunflower management' or **groupthink**. That is where the team agrees with the boss because it's the thing to do for a quiet life. The best discussions on planning, forecasting, and strategising, will have varying levels of crossfire, audio volume, interaction and reaction. The optimum results emerge from a variety of inputs, and the worst possible results are when there is a nodding competition around the table. This has been covered in the previous section, and is worth a further mention in this context.

> What can the future hold, and are you ready to meet it? Better still are you prepared to design it?

In organisations such as Credit Unions, there is a sense of stability, and all stakeholders, particularly the members, value this. However, the management and board are responsible for safely steering the ship through rough waters. This calls for some assumptions that the waters may be calm now but become choppy in time. Scenarios allow us to confront established beliefs in a less threatening way, and consider the outcomes for the business should some of these beliefs be negatively impacted.

Most leaders will set out a clear specific path and rally the troops around that objective. Scenarios do not call for increased doubt in the direction or strategy, rather they point to possible obstacles internally and externally that may be faced in the pursuit of the strategy.

It would have been of enormous benefit to the country if during the Celtic Tiger economic bubble, the financial sector had some leadership that understood scenario planning. Rather than blindly skipping up the yellow brick road, scenarios would have prompted the leadership to test the assumptions that certain banks and insurance companies were sufficiently capitalised, and that the construction industry was on a never ending upwards trajectory.

When presenting scenarios it is recommended to show more than three so it forces a real choice. Be prepared to be completely wrong, as it's not your function to accurately predict major swings in business or economic factors. You are merely broadening the minds of those who are responsible for agreeing the strategy.

The following are some suggested scenario modelling tools to prompt or guide you in scenario planning:

- Decide on the time frame you are considering. Perhaps look at the next five years, which is considered the medium term.

- What issues are likely to have the most impact on your Credit Union? You can use the **PESTEL** factors to help identify the likely drivers that would have the most significant impact.
  o **P**olitical
  o **E**conomic
  o **S**ocial
  o **T**echnological
  o **E**nvironmental
  o **L**egal

- Outline broad contingency plans to cope with some of the more likely outcomes. At the very least, consider the impact of these outcomes and then decide to dismiss them as highly unlikely or significant enough to warrant a small team looking further at the effects of such a scenario.

Now that you have peered into the possible futures, it is advisable to develop some warning system to announce the imminent arrival of one or more of your scenarios. Such systems are in place to predict natural disasters like earthquakes and tsunamis. There is little point in being one of the first to realise that an economic tsunami is heading your direction, unless you have the ability to act quickly. You can refer to this as your **emergency infrastructure**.

Your risk officer will be familiar with the concept of identifying the probability and impact of various risks, and no doubt you have a fully functioning risk management tool in operation which is regularly reviewed by the board. Although somewhat similar in approach, scenario analysis is at the higher strategic level as it positions the strategic plan into the midst of possible future scenarios, and asks you to examine your state of readiness for such scenarios.

As mentioned in the section on strategic leadership, one of the most valued attributes of todays CEOs is the ability to recognise trends and act accordingly. Scenario analysis is one of the tools to assist you and your team in developing that attribute.

Reader's notes... ✑

> Give me six hours to chop down a tree
> and I will spend the first four
> sharpening my axe.
>
> *Abraham Lincoln*

Define Culture and Capabilities

Organisational culture is often described as 'the way things are done around here'. This implies that there are many assumptions that are taken for granted, and there are behaviours that people display in relation to issues they face, all underpinned by an organisational context. To behave in any other way is to display signs that you do not fit into the organisation.

Organisational culture has a significant role to play when influencing the success, or otherwise, of any changes to the Credit Union strategy. It can be the anchor that holds the organisation in one direction when it is being steered in another path. Or it can be the engine that enables execution of the agreed strategies. Either way, it is one of the biggest influencers, and so it is useful to have a deep understanding of culture.

Edgar Schein, a renowned professor on organisational psychology and management, explains that **culture is to a group what personality or character is to an individual.** We can see the behaviours that exist but we cannot see the forces underneath that cause certain kinds of behaviour. It was Schein who is credited with coining the phrase **'the way things are done around here'.**

The reason we look at culture is that strategy and culture go hand in hand. **When we define our strategy, we must**

ensure that the culture supports it. Peter Drucker's famously remarked **'Culture eats strategy for breakfast'.** It is also said that culture eats structure for lunch! Understanding the culture is an important step to setting a strategy and the supporting structures.

Other organisations may copy your strategy, but they can never copy your culture; therefore **your culture is the key source of sustainable competitive advantage.** This is an important point to factor into your thinking. There is often very little difference between one organisation and another, especially in the financial services sector where each is basically selling money. Sustainability depends on **differentiation**, and differentiation depends on your Credit Union **culture.** Although you may talk about culture, it really is a difficult concept to explain to others.

In an attempt to understand culture it is useful to imagine a lily pond as described by Williams and Dobson. The pond is deep and the lilies float on the water. The visible behaviours are above the water, the attitudes and values are below the water and barely visible, and the deep-rooted beliefs are below the silt which are rarely changeable, or may be changeable over time.

Behaviours

The behaviours are the ways the Credit Union operates and what is seen by people from inside and outside the organisation. Behaviours includes how we are structured, and

149

controlled, our routines, the form of language used, reward systems, office layout, job titles. The behaviours in these areas are observable manifestations of our culture.

The 'Lily Pond' of Culture and Behaviour

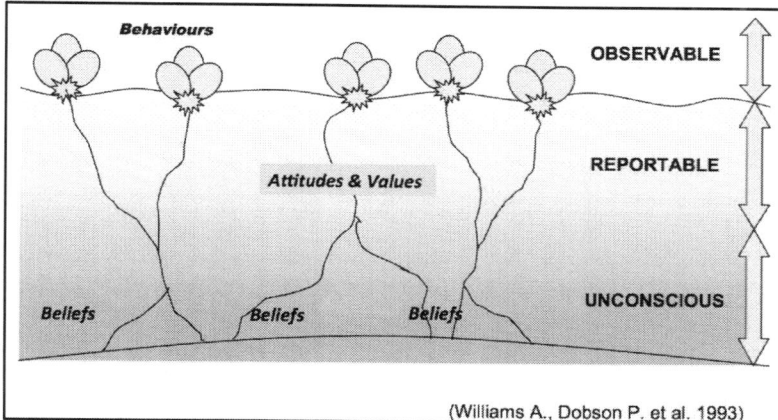

(Williams A., Dobson P. et al. 1993)

Sourced at eprints.qut.edu.au

Values and Attitudes

Slightly below the surface are the attitudes and values of the Credit Union and the individual employees. It is useful to occasionally look beneath the uncovered values and discover individual underlying values, which may be in contrast to the group values. This is normal, as individuals have their own personal values, yet they will adopt the **group values** and exhibit behaviours in line with the group expectations and norms.

Beliefs

We unconsciously develop our beliefs over our lifetime and through our experiences. Given that these drive our values and ultimately our actions and behaviours, it is acknowledged that cultural change is a long-term aspiration, if indeed it is an aspiration at all.

The lily pond image is a reminder that the behaviours we encounter are more likely to be the result of the individuals' deep-rooted beliefs rather than any recent interaction or personnel development exercises. All the meetings, training courses, mentoring and speeches have only a fleeting impact on the individual's beliefs. However, over time, these beliefs may evolve and serve as shortcuts for guiding actions and making decisions.

> Culture eats strategy for breakfast, lunch and dinner

Competitive Advantage

There is another side to this coin, which I mentioned briefly, and that is, culture is the key source of sustainable competitive advantage. To have a competitive advantage it must be **rare, valuable, and not easy to substitute**. If it is in abundant supply, or of little value, or can be replaced with an alternative or substitute, then it is certainly not sustainable. Your Credit Union's culture and the employees' beliefs, attitudes and behaviours will be the source of your Credit Union's competitive advantage.

A sustainable competitive advantage is one that cannot be eroded over time. It is the reason why members chose to do business with you and why they continue to prefer to deal with you over and above any other supplier of financial services. Your advantage must be more powerful than your competitors' low interest rates, better than the instant access to cash by moneylenders and internet lenders, and must be able to withstand the million dollar budgets being spent by mainstream banks to entice your members to do business with them.

If you do not have a competitive advantage – don't compete. The first step in making any strategy real and relevant is figuring out the big 'aha' in order to either retain or develop a sustainable competitive advantage. This 'aha' is the unique ingredient that enables your Credit Union to win in a crowded market place. And all employees should know what the 'aha' is.

There are only two sources of competitive advantage. The first is to have a monopoly on your product or service. You see this with some pharmaceutical products and medical devices companies where the manufacturer is the only supplier for an agreed timeframe following a successful patent filing and product launch. This is where there is no competition, and there is clearly a distinct advantage at play here.

The other is where the business has access to resources that no other competitor has. Sometimes this is access to an oilfield, or an abundance of fertile land, or perhaps access to unique skills. Those skills could be scientific, technological, managerial, or in your Credit Union's case it may be the culture of the organisation and the capabilities of the individuals who serve your members. It could also be the **level of trust** that your members have in the Credit Union that they could never have in another organisation, and this is fostered by the fact that the Credit Union was built by good people in the community over many years.

You don't always recognise trust as a competitive advantage, yet trust is the source of such a strong advantage that it should never go unnoticed. Trust is not easily earned and is a valuable quality. You take advice from a trusted friend, and you trust different organisations with your entire life savings. The level of trust you have with your members is an opportunity to strengthen your relationship with them. This is not only a competitive advantage, but is a highly ethical endeavour and dovetails with the core principles of the Credit Union movement. It is also a factor that can enable you to sustain that advantage over your competitors, into the long term.

In a survey of 9,000 bank consumers across nine countries published in August 2015, people rated **trust** (as in safety, security, reliability, transparency and fairness) as the key driver that separates highly satisfied consumers from less satisfied ones (Capco.com). Is there any other provider of financial services in your market place who can claim to offer the same level of fairness and transparency as your Credit Union?

153

So, when you look at the culture and then the people behind that culture, you place a high value on your employees as the delivery system for the trust, fairness and other positive attributes. From a strategy perspective you need to ask the questions that Jim Collins asks. Consider the CEO as the bus driver, and the Credit Union as the bus. The driver announces where you are and where you are going, how you are going to get there and who is going with you. Collins emphasises the importance of continuously asking **'First who, and then what?'**

- Have you the right people on the bus?
- Are the right people in the right seats?
- Have you got the wrong people off the bus?

You can then develop people into bigger seats and plan for succession. Once the right people are in the right seats, it becomes less of a question of where you are headed, and more a question of how far you want to go.

Collins firmly believes that setting out the organisation's destination before addressing the seats on the bus is folly. This is a question for all Credit Unions and all businesses, and you need to ask if you are embarking on a journey with the right resources. Is the culture of the Credit Union aligned to the task in hand, and has the Credit Union the capabilities to execute the strategic plan? No doubt you will have some great people in your organisation, so **be sure to put your best employees on the biggest opportunities, rather than on the biggest problems**.

154

I love the story of when President John F Kennedy was visiting a NASA site and met a janitor who was sweeping the floor. Kennedy asked the janitor 'And what's your job here?' The reply was 'Mr. President, I'm helping to put a man on the moon'. That response says so much about the culture of the organisation, and how individuals can connect their work to the strategic plan.

There are so many businesses where the employee is simply just doing a job, and is unconnected with the bigger picture. What a shame for the individual that they don't see themselves as a key contributor to building something great. And an even greater shame for the organisation that is unable to tap into the potential commitment and energy of that individual.

If 'the way things are done around here' is not conducive to the future success of your Credit Union, you will need to begin the task of reshaping the culture, however difficult that might be, and however long it might take.

155

Reader's notes...

We are all here on earth to help others;
What on earth the others are here for I don't know.

W H Auden

Execution

Why is it that so many initiatives, plans, strategies and objectives fail to be executed on time or at all? You start out with the very best of intentions, the team is with you in every respect, and off you go. A year or two later you can't quite fathom why so much of the vision has not materialised. Everyone in the Credit Union signed up for it. The board gave its assent and had great expectations. Yet something got between the plan and the execution.

Various surveys indicate that between 60% to 80% of companies fall far short of the targets expressed in their strategic plans. This is a staggering statistic. It is no comfort whatsoever to know that so many other organisations fail to deliver. But now you know that you need to be in the top 20% of organisations when it comes to delivering on the plan. Some of the reasons quoted for this shortfall are listed below. How does your Credit Union compare?

• Most organisations do not have formal systems to execute their strategy.

• Only 40% link their budgets to strategy.

• Only 30% link incentive compensation to strategy.

• Less than 10% of employees report that they understand their company's strategy.

157

- The research suggests that 85% of executive leadership teams spend less than one hour per month discussing their unit's strategy, with 50% spending no time at all (Kaplan & Norton 2005).

There is clearly a disconnect between strategy formulation and strategy execution. When we look at the singular result that less than 10% of employees are aware of, or do not understand the company strategy, it becomes a challenge for them to implement the strategy. If this is the case in your Credit Union you have an uphill struggle, and like those 60% to 80% of companies in the survey you will likely fail at reaching the targets expressed in your strategic plan.

'The best-laid plans of mice and men often go awry'
Robert Burns
1785

Kaplan and Norton suggest some tasks to help you address this information gap.

1. Create and manage a **balanced scorecard**. This single page document should identify performance targets from the strategic plan and act as a communications tool for all employees.

2. **Align the strategies** of each business unit, support functions, and external partners, to the broad Credit Union strategy. Actively manage this alignment by developing scorecards across the Credit Union functions.

3. Management team and board to take sufficient time to **review strategy regularly** in order to make adjustments to the strategy and its execution.

4. Developing strategy should **not be a one time annual** event.

5. **Effective communication** to employees about strategy, targets, and initiatives is vital if employees are to contribute to the strategy execution.

6. **Manage strategic initiatives** separately from routine operations. Responsibility for managing initiatives that already have a natural home should remain with the associated unit or function.

With the above points considered it should fall to the CEO to ensure that each element of the strategic plan has a manager or senior member of staff who will take ownership of that element. Someone to accept responsibility for executing that initiative or objective within budget and on time.

As mentioned above, once the plan is completed and ownership in place, the next step is to ensure that the employees are ready. There can be no doubt that this is a fundamental step to ensuring successful execution of the plan.

People prefer bite size chunks rather than the full-blown plan, as it is easier to digest. So a strategy must be broken down into small executable bites. A simple example is to explain how merely walking a member to their car is contributing to the

159

strategy and the brand. Or being there in the rain with an umbrella when the member steps out of their car is a powerful way of contributing to the plan.

The big picture is made up from lots of smaller pictures, and each employee should be able to clearly see their daily actions contributing to the overall strategy. And at the risk of being repetitive, they need to understand what the big picture is in order to make the connections!

There are three broad areas when we talk about strategy. The first two will have little or no input from the staff. However the third area is where all employees get involved.

1. **Analysis** of trends, financials, member profiles, SWOT, PESTEL, competitors, and more.

2. **Choices** to be made on segmentation decisions, member value proposition, pricing. This is beautifully referred to as; **where do we want to play, and how do we want to win**. If you would like an excellent read on this subject I can recommend Lafley and Martin's *'Playing to Win, how strategy really works'*.

3. **Actions** from marketing, human resources, operations, and processes. Many Credit Unions will not have a human resources department, but I am certain there will be humans, and their line managers will need to ensure that their actions are aligned to the strategic plan.

To summarise this section, it is fair to say that most plans do not come to fruition. This is partly caused by unforeseen or external influences. It is also due to our own failure to plan the execution as well as planning the plan. This takes some extra effort, and if you agree that it is worth the effort, you will put the time in and have a better chance of success. After all, you are consuming many hours of valuable board and management time in piecing together your strategic plan. You should use whatever tools are at your disposal to ensure it is executed as fully as possible.

Reader's notes... ✍

If you think you can do a thing
or think you can't do a thing,
you're right.

Henry Ford

Strategic Plan Contents

I know that every Credit Union has its own view on what headings to include in a strategic plan. This book would be somewhat incomplete without a reference to contents, and forgive me if you see nothing new here or if you totally disagree. The strategic plan should not be a homogenous document because you need to create it, develop it, and totally own it. In fact you will adapt it to the particular challenges and opportunities of your own Credit Union.

Each CEO and board will have their own opinions on what the priorities are and in a perfect world, no two strategic plans would be identical.

So the following headings are nothing more than a guide as to what could be included in your next strategic plan:

1. Executive summary
2. Your vision for the next five years (or longer)
3. Your mission statement
4. A statement of your Credit Union values
5. Value proposition explaining your sustainable competitive advantage
6. Situation analysis (SWOT and PESTEL)
7. Stakeholder relationships and mapping
8. The business model and details of
   a. Products and services
   b. Members and customers
   c. Financials

163

    i.   Balance sheet structure
    ii.   Cost structure
    iii.   Funding model
    iv.   Revenue model and pricing
    v.   Reserves model
    vi.   Loan loss provisioning for current and future losses

  d. Human resources
  e. Risk management and compliance
  f. Best practice and benchmarking
  g. Future scenarios and options for growth
  h. Stress testing chosen options
  i. Commentary on merger options

9. Priorities, goals, objectives and targets
10. Planning and assumptions
11. Technology, current position and any details of proposed enhancements
12. Brand positioning and brand equity
13. Distribution channels
14. Outline marketing plan
15. Organisational structure with key functions and brief profiles, key skills and experience, performance recognition system, industrial relations, culture definition.
16. Governance
17. Key performance indicators
18. Execution system & tools

When a stakeholder reads the strategic plan it is not always clear as to **how** certain goals will be attained, or **why** the Credit Union is aiming in a certain direction. For these reasons it is useful to include some background information that may be obvious to you, but not so obvious to the reader.

It will be rare to see a Credit Union strategic plan with all the above headings, and in many cases there will be references to the different points albeit grouped together for convenience and clarity.

Most CEO's and managers will have already written several strategic plans, and you will have your own way of stamping your personality on this Credit Union document. The foregoing headings are merely to act as a prompt in the event that you have overlooked an element that you wish to include in your next review of your strategic plan with your board.

The Central Bank of Ireland issued a 389-page handbook in January 2016, which includes the requirement under the Credit Union Act to prepare a strategic plan. This handbook offers guidance on:

- The minimum contents to be included
- Preparation of the strategic plan
- Strategies for achieving the strategic objectives
- Maintaining adequate resources
- Monitoring and reviewing the plan

It is worth reading that section of the handbook in conjunction with this book. As with all mentions, you will find a reference to that publication in the bibliography at the end of this book.

Reader's notes...

Unless commitment is made, there are only
promises and hopes; but no plans.

Peter F Drucker

Your Strategy Toolbox

For the benefit of the few readers who find this topic (and the book) of great interest, I have set out some of the tools that strategists and academics use to address the topic of strategy. Why not take a closer look at a few of these and dip your toe in the water of a few more?

Ansoff's Growth Grid

This is the product/growth matrix that can be used to generate how a Credit Union might grow. First published in 1957 by Harvard Business Review, it has given businesses a quick and simple way to develop a strategic approach to growth.

		PRODUCTS	
		EXISTING	NEW
MARKETS	EXISTING	Market Penetration	Product Development
	NEW	Market Development	Diversification

167

BHAG (pronounced Bee-Hag)

Your Credit Union's Big Hairy Audacious Goal. What is it that you can be the best in the world at? How will you define in a few words, exactly what you are trying to achieve. One massive goal that everyone can aspire to achieving, and that you are passionate about. Clearly it must be directly aligned to your Credit Union's strategic plan, otherwise it's inappropriate.

Blue Ocean Strategy

This is where your Credit Union identifies a new niche market, and provides an offering that makes the competition irrelevant. W. Chan Kim and Renée Mauborgne developed blue ocean strategy. They observed that companies usually tend to engage in head-to-head competition in search of sustained profitable growth. Yet in today's overcrowded industries competing head-on results in rivals fighting over a shrinking profit pool. Lasting success increasingly comes, not from battling competitors, but from creating blue oceans of untapped new market spaces, ripe for growth.

Boston Matrix

A model to help your Credit Union analyse your portfolio of business and your brand. Generally the number one and number two market leaders have the profit margins and any business below fourth in the market is just waiting to die off. You need to invest in the stars, kill off the dogs, keep just a few of the problem children and the cash cows will fund the lot. The matrix looks at high or low market growth on the one side, and high or low market share on the other side. The

Credit Union cash cows are likely to be the regular personal borrowers who are not rate sensitive and borrow frequently without being prompted.

		Market Share	
		High	Low
Growth of Market	High	STAR	QUESTION MARK / PROBLEM CHILD
	Low	CASH COW	DOG

Core Competencies

According to the core competence model, which was designed by Gary Hamel and C. K. Prahalad, organisations can move into new markets and market growth possibilities more easily by using their core competencies. The reason you define core competencies is to better understand the available specialised knowledge that is difficult to imitate by other organisations. Unlike Porter's 'outside-in-view' this theory focuses on the 'inside-out-view'.

Doblin Model

The Doblin model looks at the ten types of innovation. From configuration of the concept through to the member experience. You can use the ten types to help your innovation efforts in many ways. It can be a diagnostic tool to assess how you're approaching innovation internally, it can help you analyse your competitive environment, and it can reveal gaps and potential opportunities for doing something different and upending the market.

Eagle Eye

It is useful to have an individual who is looking out for the future of your Credit Union. It could be an individual who is close to retirement. Ideally someone who is/was a successful business person in the locality, who is not a board member, but someone willing and able to offer sound advice based on experience. This person would not be constrained by culture or fear of reprisal and can put forward challenging observations for consideration.

Edward De Bono: Six Thinking Hats

Edward De Bono (born 19 May 1933) is a physician, psychologist, author, inventor and consultant. He originated the term lateral thinking, wrote the book Six Thinking Hats and is a proponent of the teaching of thinking as a subject in schools. There are several short videos on YouTube that will challenge you and your team on your ability to think. If you think you are a good thinker, think again!

Effectiveness Efficiency Grid

This relates to how you manage your own time and that of your employees. There are those employees or teams who 'do things right', and these are high on efficiency but low on effectiveness. Then there are those who are 'doing the right things', and they are highly effective but lacking in efficiency. The ideal quadrant to be in is 'doing the right things right'. It is worth reflecting on some of your Credit Union operations and assessing how much time is spent in each quadrant. A good place to start is to look at your own management meetings, and make a call on the levels of efficiency and effectiveness. Can you score 100% on your effectiveness as well as your efficiency?

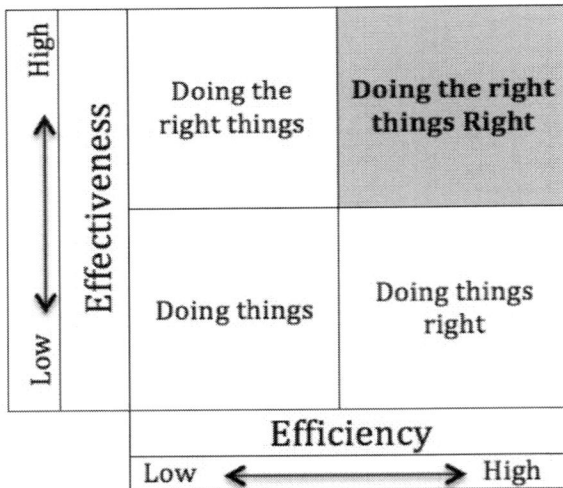

Ekvall model of creative climate

Goran Ekvall, professor emeritus of organisational psychology at the University of Lund, Sweden spent many years looking at the organisational climatic dimensions, which affects organisational creativity. The three broad dimensions are Resources, Motivation, and Exploration. He questions many aspects of the organisation and asks these five questions about your Credit Union:

- How important is creative behaviour and performance in your organisation?
- How does your team rate on the ten facets?
- What happens in your environment now that is helpful and supportive to your creativity?
- What happens in your environment now that is hindering your creativity?
- How might you improve the climate for creativity?

Emotional Intelligence (EQ)

Can you read how others are feeling? Emotional intelligence is the 'something' in each of us that is a bit intangible. It affects how we manage behaviour, navigate social complexities, and make personal decisions that achieve positive results. Emotional intelligence is made up of four core skills that pair up under two primary competencies: personal competence and social competence. Decades of research now point to emotional intelligence as the critical factor that sets star performers apart from the rest of the pack. This is considered one of the essential tools from the toolbox.

Greiner's Growth Model

The 'Greiner Curve' is a useful way of thinking about the crises that organisations experience as they grow. By understanding it, you can quickly comprehend the root cause of many of the problems you're likely to experience in a fast

172

growing business. More than this, you can anticipate problems before they occur, so that you can meet them with pre-prepared solutions.

Verne Harnish covered the topic of organisational growth in his book '*Scaling up. How a few companies make it....and why the rest don't*'.

Harvard Business Review Magazine

If I had to choose one monthly subscription to a magazine it would have to be the HBR. No other publication will give you the volumes of fresh thinking from a management perspective. Every management topic under the sun is covered. The contributors are the best and the brightest and you are guaranteed to be inspired or educated with each month's edition. You can leave these magazines for your team to browse through, as they never really go out of date.

And don't forget to subscribe to the podcast so you can listen to it on the way to work or while you go for your walk.

Hrebiniak Model of Strategy Execution

Many models have been created to design strategy. Hrebiniak's model focuses on how to implement strategy. It helps you see a logical view of the organisation and its component parts, see how the parts integrate and relate to each other, and identify the parts of the organisation that need to change in order to execute a strategy. It also helps you to plan the changes that need to be made and allocate resources to support the change.

173

Incumbent Advantage

'Failing to capitalise on the Incumbent's Advantage is to invite almost certain competitive disruption' (MacMillan 2008). Where it is evident that an invader is making inroads on a profitable segment of your Credit Union business, you should use your superior knowledge of your members to enhance your offering and deliver enough value to recapture the segment. This tactic implies that you have a knowledge advantage, particularly of the member segments that generate significant revenue streams. Any such invasion attempt should prompt the Credit Union to gain further insights into member loyalty to ensure that other segments are not vulnerable.

Kaplan & Norton Balanced Scorecard

The balanced scorecard is a strategic planning and management system that is used extensively in business and industry, government, and non-profit organisations worldwide to align business activities to the vision and strategy of the organisation, improve internal and external communications, and monitor organisation performance against strategic goals. It was originated by Dr Robert Kaplan (Harvard Business School) and Dr David Norton as a performance measurement framework that added strategic non-financial performance measures to traditional financial metrics to give managers and executives a more 'balanced' view of organisational performance. If your Credit Union has not devised and adopted a Balanced Score Card, you should do so now. It is an excellent communication tool for board, management and staff, as it enables you to link the short-term actions to the long-term strategy for your business. I would go so far as to suggest that each business unit in your Credit Union should have a balanced score card that feeds into the overall monthly one. Each business unit should know how they are progressing against pre agreed objectives, and all linked back to the strategic plan.

Key Performance Indicators (KPI's)

KPI's are useful to see at a glance if you are on target or not. Be careful not to use the first dozen KPI's that you might traditionally opt for. Finding the right ones can take time, and you may need to brainstorm them. Try to use KPI's in the context of teams, and use the ones that encourage the right behaviours. They must be understandable to all employees, and communicated to the entire team as often as possible. KPI's will form part of the balanced score card results.

Kotter's 8 Phases of Change

Over four decades, Dr John Kotter observed countless leaders and organisations as they were trying to transform or execute their strategies. He identified and extracted the success factors and combined them into a methodology, the award-winning 8-Step Process. Step 1 is to create a sense of urgency around the need for change, and this is so true if people are going to buy into the need for change. Study all eight steps to develop your understanding of change dynamics, and increase your chances of successfully implementing strategic shifts in your Credit Union.

175

John Kotter 8 Steps to Successful Change	
Step 8	Institutionalize the change
Step 7	Consolidate and build on the gains
Step 6	Create short term wins
Step 5	Empower people to act on the vision
Step 4	Communicate the vision
Step 3	Develop a clear shared vision
Step 2	Create a guiding coalition
Step 1	Establish a sense of Urgency

Lewin's Force Field Analysis

Force Field Analysis is a useful decision-making technique. It helps you make a decision by analysing the forces for and against a change, and it helps you communicate the reasoning behind your decision. Kurt Lewin's Force Field Analysis is a powerful strategic tool used to understand what is needed for change in both corporate and personal environments. It may appear as a simplistic approach, but it can be a powerful tool to weigh up the forces that will restrain or drive the change, and it's so easy to understand.

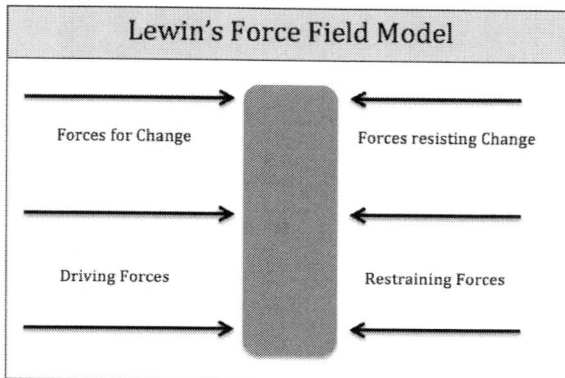

Lewin's Force Field Model

Forces for Change — Forces resisting Change

Driving Forces — Restraining Forces

McKinsey Insights

McKinsey & Company is a global management consulting firm that serves leading businesses, governments, non governmental organisations, and not-for-profits. They help their clients make lasting improvements to their performance and realise their most important goals. I recommend them as a source of up to date thinking, informing management on the global economy. The McKinsey App is a handy tool, which covers strategy as one of their core topics. And it is worthwhile signing up to their quarterly overview. This company has 9,000 consultants, 2,000 research and information professionals, and 1,400 partners.

McKinsey 7-S Framework

This framework is used to detect and resolve organisational problems. It was developed by Tom Peters and Robert Waterman who later wrote the bestseller *'In search of excellence'*. Each of the seven elements is interconnected resulting in knock-on effects if any one element is changed. The three hard elements are:

- Structure
- Strategy
- Systems

And the four soft elements are:

- Style
- Staff
- Skills
- Shared values

177

A successful Credit Union will ensure that all seven elements work together towards achieving the strategic objectives.

Mintzberg Emerging Strategy

There are only two people whose ideas must be taught to every MBA student in the world: Michael Porter and Henry Mintzberg.

Mintzberg suggests that the traditional way of thinking about strategy implementation focuses only on deliberate strategies. He claims that some organizations begin implementing strategies before they clearly articulate mission, goals, or objectives. In this case strategy implementation actually precedes strategy formulation.

Mintzberg calls strategies that unfold in this way emergent strategies. Implementation of emergent strategies involves the allocation of resources even though an organisation has not explicitly chosen its strategies.

Most organisations make use of both deliberate and emergent strategies. Whether deliberate or emergent, however, a strategy has little effect on an organisation's performance until it is implemented.

Any one of Mintzberg's several books on strategy would be a worthwhile read.

Performance Appraisals

These have to be part of your strategy toolbox, because you intend to deliver on the strategic plan through the efforts and commitment of the employees. I do not recommend one system over another, and there is not one best system that we know of. Most of the time the performance appraisal process does more harm than good, causing mistrust, creating emotional anguish, and is seen as a chore by the appraiser and appraisee.

You need to match the appraisal system with the Credit Union culture and develop a mechanism for giving regular honest feedback to help improve employees performance.

It should also contribute to a better understanding of the training gaps, and feed into the reward and recognition programme. Where possible utilise a performance appraisal system that looks at the behavioural traits of employees as well as the performance levels. Behaviours have as much impact on strategy if not more.

You should exercise caution when giving feedback on behaviours, as you need to be specific and give examples. Although an employee may appear to have a 'poor attitude', it is the behaviour that you discuss, because that is visible and factual.

Peter Principle

In 1969 the Peter Principle was written by Dr. Laurence J Peter, which purported that everyone in an organisation keeps on getting promoted until they reach their level of incompetence. At that point they stop being promoted. It was on the New York Times bestseller list for over a year and is

179

still in print 46 years later. This is a principle that every Credit Union CEO and manager should be aware of.

Harvard Business Review (HBR) addressed the question of managerial incompetence a decade later from the subordinates view, and concluded that employees should start with an assumption of good will, and that they have a responsibility to help the boss help them. It is up to the employee to speak up if expectations are not clear, to keep the boss informed, to fulfill commitments dependably, and to ask for help when needed. In response to these dilemmas, 'Managing your Boss' was first published in 1980 by John Gabaro and John Kotter and is still well worth a read today, particularly if you have a boss, and who hasn't?

The point of the Peter Principle is so that you are not too surprised to see individuals in a role they are unable to fill. Likewise that you be clever enough to trial an employee at the next level of responsibility before you formally promote that person to the role or position. There is a gulf of a difference between **confidence and competence**, and that is another topic for another day.

Plan on a Page

Most strategic plans are between twenty and sixty pages long, and this can be a daunting read for any stakeholder, especially an employee. Many businesses are now of the same view as Verne Harnish who says 'if you want to get everyone in the company on the same page, then you need to literally get everything on one page'. The one-page strategy allows your Credit Union to boil everything down to its simplest form and align it with your core values, purpose, a BHAG (big hairy audacious goal) and action items. Every board member, volunteer and employee should have a one page strategic plan. There is a greater chance that every individual will be singing off the same hymn sheet if there is only one sheet, and every employee has it.

Porters Five Forces

Porter's Five Forces of Competitive Position Analysis were developed in 1979 by Michael E Porter of Harvard Business School as a simple framework for assessing and evaluating the competitive strength and position of a business organisation within an industry or market.

This theory is based on the concept that there are five forces that determine the competitive intensity and attractiveness of a market. Porter's five forces help to identify where power lies in a business situation. This is useful both in understanding the strength of an organisation's current competitive position, and the strength of a position that an organisation may look to move into.

The model looks at analysing the supplier power, the power of buyers, the extent of competitive rivalry, the threat of substitutes, and the threat of new entrants. Adopting this model ensures that you are looking in the right directions to protect your Credit Union from sudden failure or failure over time. If you are not yet familiar with Porter's Five Forces, I strongly recommend that you become acquainted with it as a priority.

181

**Porters
Five Force Analysis**

Suppliers

Bargaining Power

Potential
Entrants

Threat of
Entry

Industry
Competitors

Threat of
Substitutes

Substitutes

Bargaining Power

Buyers

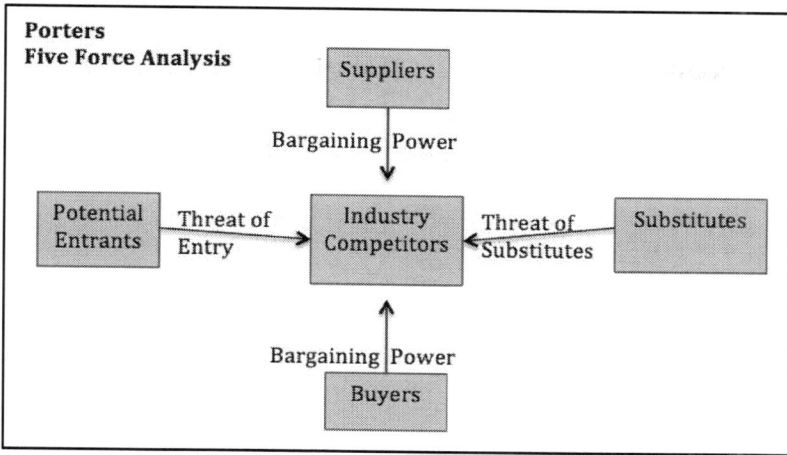

Porters Value Chain and value system

The term 'Value Chain' was used by Michael Porter in his book *'Competitive Advantage: Creating and Sustaining Superior Performance'* (1985). The value chain analysis describes the activities the organisation performs and links them to the organisations competitive position.

Value chain analysis describes the activities within and around an organisation, and relates them to an analysis of the competitive strength of the organisation. Therefore, it evaluates which value each particular activity adds to the organisations products or services. This idea was built upon the insight that an organisation is more than a random compilation of machinery, equipment, people and money. Porter distinguishes between primary activities and support activities. Primary activities are directly concerned with the creation or delivery of a product or service. Support activities relate to technology, human resource management, infrastructure and procurement.

Prahalad & Harts Bottom of the Pyramid

When CK Prahalad's book, *The Fortune at the Bottom of the Pyramid*, was published in 2004, the book made an immediate splash. Its argument was irresistible: *"The world's poorest people are a vast, fast-growing market with untapped buying power"*, Prahalad wrote, *"and companies that learn to serve them can make money and help people escape poverty, too"*.

Microsoft founder Bill Gates called the book 'an intriguing blueprint for how to fight poverty with profitability'. To some extent, the Credit Union movement adopts this view as it serves many members who could be described as poor. Although we do not need to build our business exclusively around the poorest in the community, we do realise that there are ways to serve that community without making a loss.

Shared Value

The concept of shared value relates to the operating excellence and policies that develop the competitiveness of a Credit Union while at the same time furthering the economic and social conditions in the community or common bond. The development of shared value concentrates on identifying and expanding the connections between the improvements in economic conditions and the improvement in social conditions. Whilst businesses have in the past concentrated solely on the creation of economic wealth, many are now also focusing on their impact on society. The Credit Union is in this space already, and any strategy that advances shared value is a perfect fit with the philosophy of the Credit Union movement.

Stakeholder Mapping

Stakeholder mapping helps us to see who the key blockers and facilitators of a strategy are likely to be, and consider where we may need to maintain a level of interest. It is a basic model that looks at identifying all your stakeholders, and classifying them in respect of who have most or least power, and those with a high or low level of interest in the Credit Union. Although members are powerful stakeholders, in general they have a low/medium level of interest in the Credit Union; that is, while there are no serious issues arising. They would move into the 'Key Player' category were there to be perceived problems, financial or otherwise. A proposed merger could also trigger a shift in members to the 'Key Player' category.

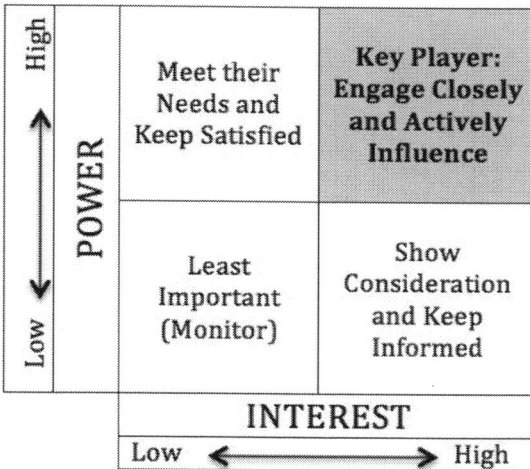

POWER	INTEREST	
High	Meet their Needs and Keep Satisfied	**Key Player: Engage Closely and Actively Influence**
Low	Least Important (Monitor)	Show Consideration and Keep Informed
	Low ⟷ High	

SMART**I** Objectives

Often when we give employees a SMART (Specific, Measurable, Attainable, Relevant, and Time bound) objective, certain actions happen and work gets done, but the net result is pointless unless there is an **Improvement.** It is the improvement that will make the difference, not the actions surrounding the objective. All credit to Tony Burke, an IMI associate who outlined this concept in the Sunday Business Post on 27 March 2016. It makes sense and managers should add the Improvement ingredient to their objectives when setting SMART objectives for their teams. What a great tool to help with the execution of the strategic plan.

Strategy Loop

It is now accepted that we should abandon the view of strategy as a linear process, in which managers chronologically draft a detailed road map to a clear destination and thereafter implement the plan. In fast-paced industries, businesses should look at strategy as an iterative loop with four steps:

1. Making sense of a situation

2. Making choices

3. Making things happen

4. Making revisions

Strategy must be capable of being added to when new information comes to light. And you can be sure that the industry and your environment will bring you surprises and new challenges on a frequent basis. Hence the need for the loop.

185

SWOT Analysis

Where would any strategic plan be without a SWOT analysis?

- **Strengths** describe the positive attributes, tangible and intangible, internal to your organisation. They are within your control

- **Weaknesses** are aspects of your business that detract from the value you offer or place you at a competitive disadvantage. You need to enhance these areas in order to compete with your best competitor

- **Opportunities** are external attractive factors that represent reasons your business is likely to prosper

- **Threats** include external factors beyond your control that could place your strategy, or the Credit Union business itself, at risk. You have no control over these, but you may benefit by having contingency plans to address them if they should occur

You can't get away from including a SWOT analysis in your strategic plan, and you should try to confine your list to those elements that are of **most importance** rather than simply develop a longer list than the last time. Summarise the two or three that are most relevant and comment on these in order to indicate to the reader that you have a strong understanding of the implications of these.

Ted Talks

TED is a non-profit devoted to spreading ideas, usually in the form of short, powerful talks of 18 minutes or less. TED began in 1984 as a conference where Technology, Entertainment and Design converged, and today covers almost all topics - from science to business to global issues - in more than 100 languages. Meanwhile, independently run TEDx events help share ideas in communities around the world. Check out the talks on strategy, design thinking, business development, community development, team management and thousands more topics. Because these are short talks they are suitable to show to staff in lieu of the occasional employee meetings. Many talks are inspiring and develop creativity.

The TEDTalks and TED Radio Hour podcasts are great company on a 30-minute drive or walk, as they are always intriguing and thought provoking.

Twelve archetypes of Brands

Successful brands have a strong sense of identity, one that mirrors the hopes and aspirations of their members or customers. But finding your voice, especially as a small business, can be difficult and expensive. Identifying your brand archetype from this list will save you time and money and connect you instantly to your audience. If you can identify what archetypes your Credit Union best fits, you're already on the path to better communication with your members.

Value Curve Analysis

A Value Curve shows graphically where differing products compete within a particular marketplace. It can then be used to significantly differentiate your product from your competitors. You can plot your Credit Union services against similar services and compare the member's perceived value on price, speed of delivery, flexibility, complexity, friendliness, add-on's, and as many other factors as you deem appropriate. This may sound complicated, but it is a fantastic way of including your employees in comparing and contrasting the values in your services and products. You will have a visual to show the results and while your Credit Union will not out-perform on every facet, you will find the elements of your Credit Union that members value highly compared to what is available elsewhere. Some of these will be obvious, and more will surprise you.

VUCA

VUCA is an acronym used to describe or reflect on the volatility, uncertainty, complexity and ambiguity of general conditions and situations. Managers should reflect on these conditions and adapt strategy accordingly. The alternative view is to decide not to work on strategy at all, given that everything is constantly changing around us. This latter approach is not recommended for Credit Unions. The term began in the 1990's and derived from military vocabulary, as did the word 'strategy'.

- **Volatility** looks at the speed and turbulence of change
- **Uncertainty** reminds you that the expected outcomes are less predictable
- **Complexity** points to the interdependencies of events internally and externally
- **Ambiguity** suggests the numerous options and possible results from those options

Wallas Model of Creativity

English social psychologist and London School of Economics co-founder Graham Wallas, outlines four stages of the creative process:

1. Preparation
2. Incubation
3. Illumination
4. Verification

This four-stage process is easy to understand and relatively easy to put into practice.

The first and last stages are left brain activities whereas the second and third stages belong to the right brain. I can attest to the difference it makes to allow for the incubation stage, especially where a small group is working on a project. It is natural to believe that most of the ideas you think of are so brilliant that they should be adopted immediately. The incubation stage is a remedy for this over confident thinking!

While confidence is a great attribute, it always amazes me how some less confident colleagues can be far more creative, given the opportunity to participate and think aloud. Wallas was

189

clearly aware of this and it is enlightening to see this model in action.

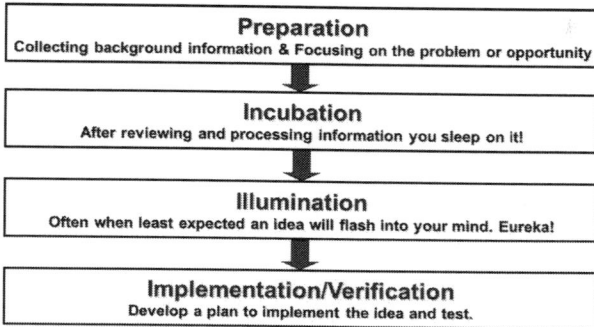

Preparation
Collecting background information & Focusing on the problem or opportunity

↓

Incubation
After reviewing and processing information you sleep on it!

↓

Illumination
Often when least expected an idea will flash into your mind. Eureka!

↓

Implementation/Verification
Develop a plan to implement the idea and test.

Reader's notes... ✍

And Then What? - Next Steps

Now that you have a broader understanding of strategy, there are a few actions I recommend as a follow on, so as to make best use of your time spent between the covers of this book.

1. First and most importantly, review the notes you made as you read through the chapters. Take those thoughts and ideas and plan how you might weave them into your Credit Union.

2. Share your thoughts and plans with your team, and look for participation in making some of the improvements you deem relevant.

3. Encourage the rest of your management team and board to get hold of their own personal edition. If needs be, make a gift of a personal copy to each of them. All proceeds are going to a national registered charity, so you are supporting a good cause as well as educating your people.

4. Understand that when you begin to think and communicate differently with your team, they will notice the difference. You need them to be on the same page, so get them involved, starting with the notes you made.

5. Remember that strategy, like life, is a journey, not a destination. Being on the right road and heading steadily

in the right direction, is so much better than travelling at speed in a random direction. So take your time to focus and share your views.

6. I am a strong believer in planning, reviewing, adapting, and re-planning. Be prepared to adjust and modify as you go.

7. Communicate the big picture to the entire team, and ask them to reflect on the impending changes. Explain where you are heading and what the Credit Union will look like if the team gets it right. Alternatively, what the future looks like if everything stays the same.

8. Ensure you have the right level of commitment and resources to deliver on the strategy. If you have less than you need of either, you need to adjust your sights downward or your resources upwards.

9. Every member of the team must know the Credit Union Mission, Values, and Vision. This is the starting point from where you build the future, and paint the picture for the team. Everything new needs to fit into this picture, so have this clear in all minds, especially the leadership team.

10. Whether you are a board member, the CEO, a manager or supervisor, or one of the team that gets things done, you have the potential to bring further success to the members you serve. They deserve the very best you can offer.

I hope that you have discovered a few gems on strategy and that your members benefit as a result.

> Do not go where the path may lead,
> go instead where there is no path and leave a trail.
>
> *Ralph Waldo Emerson*

Glossary

Term	Definition
Advocate	A member or other person who promotes your Credit Union through what they say and do.
Agile	A Credit Union that is in a position to respond quickly to changing trends.
Alliance	An association formed for mutual benefit.
ATM	Automatic Teller Machine, also known as the Hole in the Wall.
Balanced Scorecard	The balanced scorecard (developed by Kaplan and Norton) links the overall organisational goal to strategic targets and ensures performance measures extend to individual areas within the organisation.
B2C	A business serving customers or members.
BHAG	Big Hairy Audacious Goal. A key way to stimulate progress while preserving the core objectives. A huge and daunting goal – like a big mountain to climb. The point is not to find the 'right' BHAGs but to create a BHAG so clear, compelling, and imaginative that it will fuel progress and employee engagement.

Brainstorming	Process for generating creative ideas and solutions through intensive and freewheeling group discussion.
Branded Credit Card	For example a credit card offered by an airline but issued by a bank.
Business Continuity	The capability of the organisation to continue delivery of products or services at acceptable predefined levels following a disruptive incident.
Business Model	This describes how an organisation manages incomes and costs through the structural arrangement of its activities.
Capabilities	The resources and competencies that constitute an organisations overall strategic potential.
Capturing Value	Having created value, it should be possible to exchange that value with members at a fair price. The process is called Capturing value.
Cash Cow	A well-established business, product or service with a high market share in a mature market.
Choices	Looking at a range of options and opting to chose one or more over the other.

Coaching	Methods of helping others to improve, develop, learn new skills, find personal success, achieve aims and to manage life change and personal challenges.
Collaborative Response	A response from a group of people who have looked at an endeavour as a group.
Commitment	A willingness to give ones time and energy to something one believes in.
Common Bond	What each Credit Union member has in common, whether it is community or industry based.
Competitive Advantage	A condition or circumstance that puts a company in a favourable or superior business position.
Competitiveness	The ability of a Credit Union to deliver products and services in relation to the ability of other organisations to deliver similar products and services in the same market.
Compliance	The efforts to ensure that organisations are abiding by both industry regulations and government legislation.

Conflict Management	The process of limiting negative aspects of conflict while increasing the positive aspects.
Co-Operation	The action or process of working together to the same end.
Core Values	The core values are the guiding principles that dictate behaviour and action.
Creativity	The use of imagination or original ideas to create something.
Cross Company Innovation Groups	Also referred to as cross-functional teams. A group of people from different functional expertise working towards a common goal.
CUCORA	Credit Union and Co-Operation with Overseas Regulators Act 2012.
Customer Intimacy	A marketing strategy where a service supplier or product retailer gets close to their customers or members.
Customer Journey	The customer journey is the complete sum of experiences that members go through when interacting with your Credit Union and your brand.

Delivery Channels	The various ways and means by which you communicate with your members, and deliver your services to them.
Design Thinking	The process of looking for options before you look for solutions.
Dictaphone	A small hand held cassette recorder used to record speech for transcription at a later time.
Differentiation	Involves uniqueness in some dimension that is sufficiently valued by members to tolerate a price premium.
Disruption	Describes a process whereby a smaller company with fewer resources is able to successfully challenge established businesses.
Diversification	A corporate strategy to enter into a new market or industry which the business is not currently in, whilst also creating a new product for that new market.
Dog	A business unit or product or service with a low market share in a low growth market.
Durability	The amount of use one gets from a product before it becomes obsolete or deteriorates.

Emergent Strategy	The process of identifying unexpected outcomes from the execution of corporate strategy and then learning to integrate those unexpected outcomes into future corporate plans.
Empathy	The ability to understand others and share their feelings.
Enforcement	To make sure that people do what is required.
Execution	The carrying out of a plan, order, or course of action.
Expectation	A strong belief that something specific will occur.
Five Forces Framework	A framework devised by Michael Porter to help organisations identify the main sources of competition in their industry or sector.
Force field Analysis	A basic four-step process that can help identify the forces that can aid and resist efforts to make a strategic decision or plan. It can be used to analyse a number of strategic options and aid selection.

Foresight	The ability to predict what may happen in the future.
Franchisee	The one who purchases a franchise from a Franchisor, and acquires a license to use the business name and business model.
Governance	Establishment of policies, and continuous monitoring of their proper implementation, by the members of the governing body of an organisation.
Homogenised	To make something similar or uniform.
Innovation	The process of translating an idea or invention into a product or service that creates value for which the member will pay.
Insight	The ability to ascertain the true nature of a situation or something.
Internet Lenders	Those organisations that offer payday loans and instant cash, without the need to meet the customer/member.
Joint Venture	A commercial enterprise undertaken jointly by two or more parties which otherwise retain their distinct identities.

Key Performance Indicators (KPI's)	A (KPI) is a measurable value that demonstrates how effectively a company is achieving key business objectives. Organisations use KPIs to evaluate their success at reaching milestones and targets.
Lafley, Alan G	An American businessman and executive chairman of Procter & Gamble, previously serving as chairman, president and CEO. As CEO, Lafley is credited with revitalising P&G under the mantra 'Consumer is Boss,' with a focus on billion dollar brands like Crest, Tide, and Pampers. But he also brought in several new brands, like Swiffer and Febreze, by merging P&G's internal resources with outside 'open' innovation, referred to as Connect + Develop. Prior to rejoining P&G in 2013, Lafley consulted on business and innovation strategy, advising on CEO succession and executive leadership development, and coaching experienced, new, and potential CEOs. He took a commission with the US Navy as a supply officer during the Vietnam War. Afterwards, he studied at Harvard Business School, receiving his MBA in 1977.

Liquidity	Short-term investments or cash deposits on call.
Market Segments	An identifiable group of individuals, communities, or businesses sharing one or more characteristics.
Market Share	This refers to a Credit Union's portion of sales within the entire market in which it operates.
Martin, Roger	The Institute Director of the Martin Prosperity Institute at the Rotman School of Management and the Premier's Chair in Productivity & Competitiveness. From 1998 to 2013, he served as Dean. In 2013, he was named global Dean of the Year by the leading business school website, Poets & Quants. He has published 10 books the most recent of which are *'Getting Beyond Better'* written with Sally Osberg (Harvard Business Review Press, 2015) and *'Playing to Win'* written with A.G. Lafley (Harvard Business Review Press (HBRP), 2013), which won the award for Best Book of 2012-13 by the Thinkers50. He has written 21 Harvard Business Review articles.

Member Experience	The entirety of the interactions a member has with a Credit Union.
Mentoring	A relationship in which a more experienced or more knowledgeable person helps to guide a less experienced or less knowledgeable person.
Mintzberg, Henry	Took up a career in education after he had obtained a Master's degree (M.Sc.) in management (1965) and a doctorate (Ph.D.) from the MIT Sloan School of Management (1968). He is especially interested in and passionate about topics within management and business strategy. He has written over 150 articles and 15 books. He is currently professor of Management Studies at the Desautels Faculty of Management of McGill University in Montreal, Quebec, Canada.
Mission	An important task that is given to someone or a team to do.
Mission Ready	Ready to proceed in the full knowledge of what must be achieved.
Monopoly	The exclusive possession or control of the supply of or trade in a commodity or service.

Obsolescence	Something no longer in use.
Operational Excellence	A philosophy of the workplace where problem solving, teamwork, and leadership results in the ongoing improvement in an organisation. The process involves focusing on the members' needs, keeping the employees positive and empowered, and continually improving the current activities in the workplace.
PESTLE Framework	A strategic analysis tool that helps organisations to explore/anticipate external influences on their organisation or department from several perspectives: • Political • Economic • Social • Technological • Legal • Environmental
Point of Difference	Point of difference refers to the factors of products or services that establish differentiation.

Porter, Michael	An economist, researcher, author, advisor, speaker and teacher. Throughout his career at Harvard Business School, he has brought economic theory and strategy concepts to bear on many of the most challenging problems facing corporations, economies and societies, including market competition and company strategy, economic development, the environment, and health care. His extensive research is widely recognised in governments, corporations, NGOs, and academic circles around the globe. His research has received numerous awards, and he is the most cited scholar today in economics and business. While Dr. Porter is, at the core, a scholar, his work has also achieved remarkable acceptance by practitioners across multiple fields.
Proactivity (or proactive behaviours)	Refers to anticipatory, change-oriented and self-initiated behaviour in situations, particularly in the workplace.
Problem Children	Also known as question marks. They are business units or products or services in a growing market, but without a high market share.

Product Leadership	A competitive strategy that aims to build a culture of continuously bringing superior products to market.
Prototype	Someone or something that serves as a model or inspiration for those that follow later.
Realised Strategy	The actual strategy that unfolds within the organisation. This can be the outcome of a deliberate strategy; an intended strategy that has been altered (e.g. because of environmental changes or stakeholders objections); or the result of emergent strategy.
Reserves	There are different types of reserves used in financial accounting like capital reserves, revenue reserves, statutory reserves, realised reserves, and unrealised reserves. Credit Union reserves are the retained surpluses, which are maintained to shore up the business in emergency situations.
Resource Fluidity	The internal capability to reconfigure business systems and redeploy resources rapidly.

Robert, Michel	Founder and president of Decision Processes International, Inc., an internationally known consulting firm with 60 partners in 15 countries that include Caterpillar, Volvo, and FIAT. A noted speaker, he has written articles in numerous business magazines and journals. He is the author of '*The Power of Strategic Thinking*', '*Product Innovation Strategy Pure & Simple*', and '*Strategy Pure & Simple II*', and is credited with coining the term strategic thinking.
Scenario Planning	Identifying the impact of possible future scenarios.
Social Dividend	Distributing a portion of the annual surplus direct into community projects and supporting community initiatives throughout the year as required.
Stakeholder Mapping	This is used to identify stakeholder power and expectation and to predict how stakeholders may respond to a strategy.
Stakeholders	An internal or external individual or business or agency who has an interest in the Credit Union.

Star	A well-established business unit or product or service with a high market share in a growing market and, therefore, rapidly growing sales and tremendous opportunities.
Steiner, George	After high school, Steiner went to the University of Chicago, where he studied literature as well as mathematics and physics, and obtained a BA degree in 1948. This was followed by an MA degree from Harvard University in 1950. He then attended Balliol College at the University of Oxford in England on a Rhodes scholarship. After several years as a freelance writer and occasional lecturer, Steiner accepted the post of Professor of English and Comparative Literature at the University of Geneva in 1974; he held this post for 20 years, teaching in four languages. He became Professor Emeritus at Geneva University on his retirement in 1994, and an Honorary Fellow at Balliol College at Oxford University in 1995.
Strategic Offensive	Refers to those strategies that companies adopt to stay ahead of the competition rather than react to the competition.

Strategic Plan	The output from an organisation's process of defining its strategy, or direction, and making decisions on allocating its resources to pursue this strategy.
Strategic Thinking	Strategic thinking is defined as the individual's capacity for thinking conceptually, imaginatively, systematically, and opportunistically with regard to the attainment of success in the future.
Substitute	A product or service that can take the place of an existing one.
Sustainable Growth	In simple terms and with reference to a business, sustainable growth is the realistically attainable growth that a company could maintain without running into problems. A business that grows too quickly may find it difficult to fund the growth. A business that grows too slowly or not at all may stagnate.
Sustainability	The ability to continue a defined behaviour indefinitely.

SWOT Analysis	An analytical tool that can be used to help organisations establish their present situation, and evaluate potential options. • Strengths • Weaknesses • Opportunities • Threats •
Treacy, Michael	An internationally known expert on corporate strategy and business process transformation. He is pioneering a whole new approach to customer, industry, and competitive analysis. Known as Value Disciplines, Treacy's powerful concepts show how market leaders deliver exceptional value by focusing on three disciplines. He was professor at the MIT Sloane School of Management, and received his BS from the University of Toronto and his PhD from Sloane MIT.
Treasury	The financial management of the Credit Unions funds.
Turbulence	A state of confusion and disorder.

Value disciplines	A model created by Michael Treacy and Fred Wiersema describing three generic 'value disciplines' companies can adhere to. These disciplines are 1) Operational Excellence 2) Product Leadership and 3) Customer Intimacy.
Value Migration	The shift of the economic and shareholder value from the traditional models to new and emerging models. This is essentially a result of the emerging competitive offering to evolving consumer needs, which renders the earlier products obsolete.
Value Proposition	A clear statement that explains how your product solves members problems or improves their situation (relevancy), delivers specific benefits (quantified value), tells the ideal member why they should buy from you and not from the competition (unique differentiation).
Values	Important and lasting beliefs shared by members of a Credit Union on what is important and held in high esteem.

Vision	An aspirational description of what an organisation would like to achieve or accomplish in the mid-term or long-term future. It is intended to serve as a clear guide for choosing current and future courses of action.
Wiersema, Fred	In addition to being a well-known author, entrepreneur and advisor, Fred Wiersema is a visionary in the area of strategy and is also known for his contribution of the development of the value and growth disciplines. He obtained his Bachelor degree upon completing his BSc. Economics programme at the Erasmus University. Furthermore, he obtained an MA degree in Marketing from the University of Lancaster, UK. Wiersema also holds a PhD in Business Administration from Harvard University.

213

Bibliography

Ashford Castle Service awards 2015 available at
http://hoteloftheyearawards.com/top-100-hotels-worldwide-2015/

Business Model Canvas available at
http://www.businessmodelgeneration.com/downloads/business_model_canvas_poster.pdf

Capco.com *Basic Banking and Beyond: The Customer Speaks.* Available at:
http://www.capco.com/insights/capco-blog/basic-banking-beyond-the-customer-speaks

Collins, J. (2001) *Good to Great: Why some companies make the leap ... and others don't.* London: Random House.

Central Bank of Ireland. *Credit Union Handbook.* Available at
http://www.centralbank.ie/regulation/industry-sectors/credit-unions/Documents/CU%20Handbook%20–%20Full%20Handbook.pdf

EY (2013) *The evolving role of today's CFO.* Available at
http://www.ey.com/Publication/vwLUAssets/Americas_CFO_ViewsVisionInsights_062012/$FILE/Americas_CFO_ViewsVisionInsights_062012.pdf

Gabarro, J. and Kotter, J. (2008) *Managing your Boss.* Boston: Harvard Business Review Press.

Harnish, Verne. (2014) *Scaling up. How a few companies make it....and why the rest don't.* Ashburn, Virginia: Gazelles Inc

James, Geoffrey. Inc.com *8 Core Beliefs of Extraordinary Bosses.* Available at http://www.inc.com/geoffrey-james/8-core-beliefs-of-extraordinary-bosses.html

Johnson, S. (1998) *Who Moved My Cheese? An A-Mazing way to deal with change in your work and in your life.* New York: Penguin Publishing Group

Kaplan, R.S. and Norton, D.P. (2013) *The Execution Premium: Linking Strategy to Operations for Competitive Advantage.* Boston: Harvard Business Review Press.

Kaplan, R.S. and Norton, D.P. (2005) *The Office of Strategy Management.* Available at https://hbr.org/2005/10/the-office-of-strategy-management

Kaplan, R.S. and Norton, D.P. (2007) *Using the Balanced Scorecard as a Strategic Management System.* Boston: Harvard Business Review Press (July-August 2007 Pages 150-161).

Kahneman, D., Lovallo, D. and Sibony, O. *Before You Make That Big Decision...* Harvard Business Review Press, June 2011 (Vol. 89, #6, p. 50-60), Lovallo and Sibony are at dan.lavallo@sydney.edu.au and olivier_sibony@mckinsey.com

Kotter, J. and Cohen, D. (2002) *The Heart of Change. Real-Life stories of how people changed their organisations.* Boston: Harvard Business Review Press.

Kotter, J. and Rathgeber, H. (2005) *Our Iceberg is Melting. Changing and Succeeding under any conditions.* New York: Penguin Random House Publications.

Lafley, A.G. and Martin, R.L. (2013) *Playing to Win, how Strategy really works.* Boston: Harvard Business School of Publishing.

Lewin, Kurt. (1951) *Field Theory in Social Science.* Harper and Row publishers.

Marr, Bernard (2010) *What are Key Performance Questions.* Management white paper. Advanced Performance Institute. Available at http://www.ap-institute.com/chief-executive.aspx

McKinsey & Company, Global Management Consulting. Available at http://www.mckinsey.com/about-us/overview

McKinsey & Company, Global Management Consulting. *Today's CFO: Which profile best suits your company?* January 2013. Available at http://www.mckinsey.com/business-functions/strategy-and-corporate-finance/our-insights/todays-cfo-which-profile-best-suits-your-company

McMillan, Ian C. and Seldon, L (2008) *The Incumbent's Advantage*. Boston: Harvard Business Review, October 2008 (P.111-121)

Mintzberg, H. (2000) *The Rise and Fall of Strategic Planning*. Prentice Hall, Pearson Education, Financial Times

Newton, Isaac, Sir. BBC Learning English. Available at http://www.bbc.co.uk/worldservice/learningenglish/moving words/shortlist/newton.shtml

Nickols, Fred. 2012 *Strategy Definitions and meanings.* Available at http://www.nickols.us/strategy_definition.htm

Peter, L. J. and Hull, R. (2014) *The Peter Principle: Why things always go wrong.* New York: Harper Collins.

Peters, T. and Waterman, R.H. (2012) *In Search of Excellence. Lessons from America's Best-Run Companies.* New York: Harper Collins

Porter, M. (1986) *Competitive Strategy*. Boston: Harvard Business School Press.

217

Porter, M. (Nov-Dec 1996). *What is Strategy?* Boston: Harvard Business Review

Robert, M. (1993) *Strategy: Pure and Simple.* McGraw-Hill.

Rothwell, W.J. (2009) *Effective Succession Planning: Ensuring Leadership Continuity and Building Talent from Within.* Pennsylvania: American Management Association.

Roxborough Charles, Director McKinsey.com **The Use and Abuse of Scenarios.** November 2009. Available at http://www.mckinsey.com/business-functions/strategy-and-corporate-finance/our-insights/the-use-and-abuse-of-scenarios

Ruffino, Jane (21st February 2016) The Sunday Business Post. *The chip makers new goals*

Schein, Edgar H. (2010) *Organizational Culture and Leadership.* San Fransisco. John Wiley & Sons.

Schwartz, D. J. (2016) *The Magic of Thinking BIG.* London: Vermilion.

Senge, Peter M. (2006) *The Fifth Discipline: The Art & Practice of The Learning Organisation.* USA. Doubleday (a division of Random House Inc).

Shaw, George B. (First published in 1921 and republished in 2010) *Back to Methuselah.* Auckland. The Floating Press

Steiner. G. A. *Strategic Planning. What every Manager Must know.* (1979) New York: Free Press.

Slywotzky, Adrian J. (1995) *Value Migration: How to Think Several Moves Ahead of the Competition.* Boston: Harvard Business School of Publishing.

Treacy, M. and Wiersema, F. (Jan-Feb 1993). *Customer Intimacy and Other Value Disciplines.* Harvard Business Review Press

Treacy, M. and Wiersema, F. (1994). *The Discipline of Market Leaders.* Reading MA: Addison-Wesley Publishing Company

Williams, A., Dobson, P. and Walters, M. (1993) *Changing Cultures: New organisational approaches.* London: Institute of Personnel Management.

Williams, A., Dobson, P. and Walters, M. *The Lily Pond of Culture and Behaviour image.* Available at: http://eprints.qut.edu.au/7989/1/7989.pdf

219

The reader may take a bow at this point.................

If you know of a Credit Union colleague who might benefit from having his or her own book, why not buy a copy and make someone's day with a gift? You are also supporting the fight against cancer.

Thank you

Alan Shaw

.

Printed in Great Britain
by Amazon

43914468R00129